INVESTILOSOPHY

Investment Lessons Wrapped in a Story

INVESTILOSOPHY

Investment Lessons Wrapped in a Story

Ofir Hirsh

ISBN 978-1-481-09468-9
ISBN 1-481-09468-8

Cover Art © 2000 by Ofir Hirsh
"South Pacific Dream"
www.ofirhirsh.com

CONTENTS

CHAPTER 1

CHANGING DIRECTION

L ast week I was "George". Now, I am "Jorgy".
In the past few days, I have gone through a
journey that entirely changed my approach to
investing. I also think I am in love.

If I were a more spiritual person, I would have
probably said that I experienced a few moments of
enlightenment. As I see it, I was just extremely lucky
and ready to see the beauty.

Last Thursday, during a business trip to Asia, after 2
intensive days of meetings in Singapore, I arrived at Hong
Kong International Airport, early morning local time.

My plan was to spend the entire day meeting with
a major client, and hopefully closing a deal that I've
been working on for approximately 8 months.

The tremendous growth potential of Asia is no
secret, and just like many other western firms wishing
to do business in China, I was hoping that closing the
deal with this Hong-Kong client could be my
springboard to the Chinese market, and from there,
the sky would be the limit.

Since I had no commitments or plans for the
weekend, I thought to squeeze a bit more out of my trip

and have some fun before going back home to L.A. There were no urgent business issues other than the ongoing usual ones, and nobody was waiting for me.

I just came out of a 2 year relationship that according to my ex-girlfriend ended because of my over commitment to my business and my lack of commitment to her. It ended almost a month ago, I missed her, and it was my fault.

I always wanted to take her on a vacation to an exotic destination, but it never worked out. It's been quite a long time since I've taken a vacation myself, and I thought I deserved one. I decided that if I were to close the deal, I should reward myself.

Since my head was full of business matters, I didn't have any particular dream vacation in mind. I thought of maybe spending the weekend in the Hong Kong area, visiting Kowloon and maybe even travel to Macau.

Hong Kong has a distinctive charm and rhythm, and although I've been there several times for business, I was curious to discover its other sides.

Arriving at Hong Kong Airport, I turned on my Smartphone, and there they were; 3 damned e-mails.

The first from my company, the second from the client, and the third, from the intermediary that introduced between us.

They all confirmed the same message, "The meeting is canceled!"

"Shit!" I spitted out, "I can't believe it. This is not happening to me." I didn't care about the reasons, excuses, and rescheduling attempts. I only saw in my mind one word in black and white: NO. No deal, no way, not going to happen.

It wasn't the first time, and surely enough, not the last one. It's part of the business.

You go spending your time, no guarantees that it will work, or that anyone will pay your expenses. You chase a deal, and when it takes longer, you develop higher hopes for a bigger deal that would compensate for the extra time you spent. Then, it just blows up in your face.

I was thinking about all the business, motivational, and spiritual books that I have read throughout the years. They all suggest similar slogans, either in the same or in different words:

Think positive!

What doesn't kill you makes you stronger!

Learn from your failures! Become a better person!

Be happy!

While thinking about those slogans, suddenly, one song came to my mind. So there I was, standing in the middle of the airport singing and whistling to myself the famous Monty Python song, *"Always look on the bright side of life, ta da, ta da, ta da, ta da..."*

My own method for dealing with a failure, which historically proved successful in more cases than any other method, was to celebrate.

A successful method had to be the one that brings back the good and healthy feeling. I was standing for a few moments in a corner of the terminal, where I didn't disturb anyone, just to arrange my thoughts and plan my next steps.

3

I ran in my head a few places I wanted to see or visit in Hong Kong, and tried to calculate the time needed for each trip, when out of the blue, a policeman showed up, saying to me something in Chinese.

I asked him, "Do you speak English?" And he replied politely, "Yes sir, of course I speak English, it's the 2nd official language of Hong Kong."

And just when I concluded that it would take too long to discuss with him "Why then he spoke with me in Chinese? Do I look Chinese? Does he think I should speak Chinese?" He inquired, "Are you waiting for someone?" When I replied, "I'm just thinking," he laughed, pointed to the sitting area, and told me, "This is a very good place to think, Sir."

"Why not? Let's be a good boy," I thought to myself.

I replied the policeman, "Thank you sir," and held my hands together near my chest. I wasn't sure if I did it correctly, but he smiled, and I translated it as, "OK man, we are cool."

I sat down heavily, placing the laptop bag on top of the garment bag, in my traditional arrangement.

While sitting there, I quickly went through the financial news and logged-in to my on-line brokerage account to check my portfolio, as I always do.

Then I brought up in my mind all the data about the situation I was in; the location, the time, "Do I need a sleep? Food? Shower?" It was just few days in Hong Kong, and although not exactly a survival game, I wanted to be well prepared.

CHANGING DIRECTION

While I sat there thinking, I kept staring at the departing flights board, names of cities around the world, flight numbers etc.

The screen seemed homogenous and quiet. One word though kept growing bigger and bigger, "Honolulu...Honolulu...Honolulu".

"Wow," I said and smiled to myself, "Aloha Honolulu!"

I always wanted to be in Hawaii. Ever since I was a teenager, I always dreamt of Hawaii; the waves, the surfing, and the girls...

"That was long ago," I thought to myself, when I still had long hair, and not even a clue of what I was going to do with my life. Now I'm a grown up, I know who I am and what I do, and I like it, but I still have this long time dream ...Hawaii.

I began singing to myself, *"It's now or never..."* and simultaneously I tried to translate this fantasy into what I should do next in order to...

MAKE IT REALITY

"If the flight is full, I might chicken out, forget all about it, and spend a few days in Hong Kong as I originally planned. If there's even one available seat just for me, it's a sign. God knows what sign, but then I go."

I went on-line and Bingo, I booked it and still had time to grab something to eat. Next, I was on the plane, smiling like a child, "Hawaii, here I come, don't cry for me Argentina." I was tired but couldn't sleep. "What will tomorrow bring?"

KAUAI

I consider myself a lucky person in general, but when it comes to who sits next to me on the plane, I usually don't have much luck.

This time, I had a snoring man next to me. He slept with his mouth wide open most of the flight, and woke up, only forty minutes before we landed, when the crew announced the upcoming landing on the speakers.

From the little conversation we had, I learned that he is a native Hawaiian. His family has always lived on the same land and grows Coffee and all kind of tropical fruits for their living.

However, he mentioned, he is not from Oahu, but from Kauai, which as he explained to me, is the oldest island of Hawaii, the greenest, and the best for surfing.

I told him that I've heard about the "Pipeline" in Oahu and about the "Jaws" in Maui, and he replied dismissively, "You're just an enthusiastic Hauli (a white person in Hawaii). You know nothing about waves."

I found him a bit rude, but as I didn't want to offend a stranger, I politely said, "Thanks for your recommendations," thinking to myself that just like every child believes that his mother's food is the best, even if she cooks pasta with ketchup, most people believe that the place where they live is the best, the most beautiful, or in our case, has the best waves in Hawaii.

When we landed in Honolulu, I turned on my Smartphone and searched for info on Kauai. Obviously, just like in most searches of touristic destinations, I was immediately bombed with TMI (too much information).

I looked at the images of Kauai, and what caught my attention the most, was the magnificent view of the Na Pali Coast cliffs.

I didn't bother to read further about surfing spots and immediately made up my mind.

I looked around, and to my left, I saw the "Aloha Airlines" counter, with a Hawaiian girl standing behind it, wearing a white flowers necklace.

I booked a flight and there I was again, on another plane, smiling like a child.

During the short flight, I praised myself for being spontaneous and decisive.

Then I thought what an idiot I was, going to Hawaii with a garment bag full of suits and a laptop.

Surfing in Hawaii was my dream, but in reality, I didn't surf for almost 2 years. "Shame on you!" I blamed myself.

Yes, the family always comes first, and the business is always demanding, but after all, I live in Los Angeles, minutes from great surfing spots, "What's wrong with Topanga or Malibu beach?" "Why is it, that if it's closer, it's less desirable?"

My curiosity led me to many interesting places around the world, and I always felt the urge to explore more, even if it's an ugly place or a boring one. Just let it be new.

The plane landed in Lihue Airport, Kauai. It was almost dark, but I could see the mountainous topography of the island, a few short minutes before we landed.

I was exhausted. Taxi, any hotel, a shower, and saying goodbye to the world for a few hours of rest.

TO THE WATER

I woke up and my heart was beating fast.

In my dream, I was back in my high school years. I was surfing with my friends. We were purely happy. Whenever there were waves, we ran away from school to the beach, to surf.

When there were no waves, we always had the same discussion, "Are there real places where there are always waves?" Each of us quoting a cousin, an uncle, the father of a neighbor saying that, "In Hawaii, there are waves all year round."

"I'm here," I realized. "In a hotel room, in Kauai. It's Friday morning, and my flight back is on Monday afternoon. I only have 3 days here. It's not much, so I'd better get going." I looked out the window and made up my mind to do everything quickly and efficiently until I am in the water, in the ocean, surfing.

Only short and necessary e-mails, quick breakfast, buy surf shorts and definitely no swimming pool. "Give me the real thing, I waited long enough."

When I asked the man in the reception if he surfs, because I need some directions, he answered, "Of course, everybody's surfing in Kauai," and recommended that I grab a taxi to Poipu Beach, where there are surfing spots for all skill levels and where I could rent a board.

I thanked him and was relieved. "Maybe after all I'm in the right place."

"I've done it." I'm on the board, lying on my belly, and paddling hard with my heavy hands, trying to gain speed before the wave breaks.

I catch it and swiftly stand up, proud like a peacock. "I am the man and I will always be."

Despite years without practice and the mediocre shape I'm in, it still runs in my blood. Thousands of hours doing the same thing don't go down the drain. I am surfing, and I love it. It's much more than just fun. I'm in my element.

After playing in the ocean and catching some nice clean waves, I'm exhausted. My arms, my breath, my back. With all due respect to the adrenaline and the incredible feeling, I am not in shape.

I went out and sat down to relax and rest a bit. After a while, I got curious and decided to look for other spots. I was strolling down the beach with the board under my arm, when I suddenly noticed an incredible and powerful wave breaking, taking 2 happy surfers with it.

I didn't hesitate, just did the most natural thing any surfer would do. I entered the water, paddling right into this action.

When I joined the line of waiting surfers, sitting like a pro on my rented board, one foreign guy shouted at me with a strange accent, "Hey, be careful of the reef! It's dangerous."

THE WAVE

I sat there for a while, trying to figure out how the wave is built and moves, where exactly it breaks, and how powerful it is. I watched other surfers charging it and riding it stubbornly. Some, with their own natural flow and others, performing popular surfing maneuvers.

I was ready to claim what is mine. I positioned myself in the best spot, took a deep breath, and started paddling.

The wave was so strong that I didn't have to keep paddling, I jumped on the board and felt an incredible power against my board, taking me and moving me at its own will.

I realized it was too big and strong to play with, so I just let go. I experienced some kind of enlightenment during what seemed like long moments of surfing.

I was so high that I forgot about the reef and crashed right into it. It was a painful wipeout.

I turned on my surviving instincts, just like when I was a teenage surfer, but this time it was brutal.

I was stuck there, standing on my knees, on the shallow water reef, and the crashing waves pushed me further onto the sharp corals.

The leash got tangled in the corals and I had a hard time untangling it. When I finally did, I managed to pull the board back to me and climb on it. I could tell that it was damaged, but I couldn't care less.

I was alone. Nobody came to my rescue and actually, I didn't expect anyone to do so. I managed somehow to get to the shore.

JEAN GLER

I was trembling, but not in panic. I tried to estimate the situation and the damage.

I remembered an interview I once saw on "Animal Planet" with a man whose leg was bitten by a shark. He said that during the first moments, he didn't feel any pain or anything missing.

I'm not sure, but I think the explanation included high levels of Adrenaline as a pain killer, giving humans the ability to keep functioning in times of a threat or danger.

I had all my parts with me, and although I started to feel some pain and burn in my knees, in general, I thought I was OK.

I took a deep breath, and although I believe that God is everywhere, I looked to the highest point in the sky and said, "Thank you God, thanks again for watching my ass when I am acting like an idiot."

Yes, now I can admit that I wasn't such a genius, or a very responsible man. I just hope these scratches will go away quickly and that no bruise marks will appear.

I am standing up slowly, trying to move my legs, feet, fingers, arms, neck, and my conclusion is that nothing is broken.

I check the board I rented, it's broken in the upper side, but still holds together, they would probably charge me for that, but who gives a shit.

The scratches start to burn, I look down at my knees, and I'm bleeding a bit. "...Hmm," I think to myself, "It's not too bad is it?"

"Hey dude, are you ok?" A clear and slow speaking voice startled me.

I turned to face the direction the voice came from and saw a hippie that looked as if he came right out of biblical times, but with a white longboard under his arm.

I looked at him surprised and replied, "Well, yes, I think I am ok."

I told him what just happened to me and he replied, "Well dude congratulations! You're probably not aware of it, but you just surfed the "Acid Drops", one of Kauai's famous surfing spots for professional surfers. Anyway, I'm looking at those scratches and must ask you; did you do the right thing?"

I didn't exactly understand what he meant by that, but before I opened my mouth, he pointed to my knees and inquired, "Did you pee on the scratches?"

"What?" I cried out, thinking I heard it wrong, "What did you say?"

He laughed, "Yes, I know it sounds a bit perverse, but these scratches might swell and become a serious inflammation if you don't pee on them. Urine is the best medicine. Iodine, alcohol, or anything else won't cure it."

"Are you pooling my leg?" I was still a bit suspicious.

"No brother," he replied patiently, "just trying to save you some pain. Welcome home, we are all friends here and need to take care of each other. I am Jeff, by the way, but my friends call me Jean Gler."

For a moment, I thought we were back to the sixties; hippies, sharing, friends. "Well, it's actually better like that," I thought to myself. Being friendly is something we abandoned in the modern world. Nobody is greeting anyone, these days, and maybe that was the reason I was surprised that he cared about me.

"Thank you dude, but what again is your nickname?"

"It's not a nickname; it is Jean Gler. It's more of a term, a concept, and a legend. You should say it with a French accent, Jean Gler!"

"OK Jean Gler," I tried to pronounce it right, "it's very nice to meet you, and I thank you again. My name is George."

"It's my pleasure George, just practice your "Jean Gler" accent, please, and if you don't mind, I will call you Jorgy, with a Brazilian accent, after the glorious Brazilian singer."

"Do you mean Jorge Ben Jor, the crazy one who sings "Un pais tropical"? Did he die?"

"No, he didn't die. He's actually doing great, and I hope to have the chance to see him in Rio de Janeiro sometime soon.

He never comes to Kauai. I think he's so happy in Brazil that he never travels. And how come you know Jorge?"

"I'm just a big fan of Brazilian music, and even if Jorge Ben Jor is not the greatest guitar virtuous as Caetano or Djavan, he is undoubtedly number one in celebrating and fooling around."

Jean Gler seemed to be pleased with me, "Well brother Jorgy, I'm not sure we should compare. Each one of them is a king in his own kingdom, and Brazil is big enough for all, but I do, however, agree with your analysis, and I'm even quite impressed. You just gained your ride if you need one."

THE RAINBOW

According to Jean Gler's instructions, I did pee on myself; I didn't wash it off, and sat outside in the back of his pickup truck.

The road was surrounded by lush green vegetation, and a tropical warm rain began to fall. I felt better because it cleaned me from the bad smell and guilt I felt before.

Well, there I was, in the back of the truck of a weirdo hippie calling himself Jean Gler. In Kauai. In Hawaii. In the pouring rain.

Suddenly, a rainbow appeared, just like that, with perfect colors, and it followed us for several minutes.

"It's a sign," I said to myself. I wasn't sure what it meant, but I was glad I saw it.

Some people can see other people's Auras. I can't. If I could see anything around this guy I just met, Jean Gler, I would say he's a decent man, with a slight disconnection from reality.

I met many hippies with long hair and a beard in my life, but this guy was different. Something in his eyes was, at the same time, both sharp and dreamy. I wondered which of the two he was. "Could he be both?" Anyway, he liked Brazilian music, and so far, he was driving slowly and safely, so I guessed I could relax.

While my mind found a quiet place to rest during the short ride, my eyes were wide open, fascinated by the intense scenery in front of them. I completely forgot about my plans, arrangements, my situation, and how I got there. I was just enjoying the endless nature.

The truck stopped in front of my hotel in Lihue. I stepped down, giving a strong and warm handshake to my new friend, Jean Gler, saying, "Thank you very much Monsieur Jean Gler. For everything. It was a spectacular ride, and, by the way, did you see the rainbow?"

"Of course my friend, there are many of them out here. Some people believe a rainbow is a sign, and so do I, but I see a sign in everything. I imagine you had a rough day, and you are probably exhausted, but if you feel like joining us for dinner, you are most welcome. It's Friday evening, we have friends coming over and a few good reasons to celebrate.

"Just tell a cab driver to take you to the "Traders Village". When you enter the village, take the right turn that goes up to "Frangipani Hill". It's the only house on that hill, so you'll find it easily, and the gate and doors are always open."

CHAPTER 2

THE TRADERS VILLAGE

While in the cab, on the way to dinner at Jean Gler's place, I kept thinking about the recent sequence of events. "I could have never imagined such a thrilling day, and it's not over yet. I want tomorrow to be as unpredictable as today was."

The cab climbed the hill, and then the driver announced, "Here we are."

I heard music and people's laughter, and I couldn't ignore the strong fragrance of the frangipani flowers in the air of the night.

I walked through the open gate when a beige Labrador jumped and barked at me. I always loved dogs, but since a cruel Bulldog bit me a few years ago, I am on the cautious side. Barking or not, "respect and suspect" is a useful approach.

Jean Gler showed up laughing at me, "Hey brother Jorgy, come in. This is Luka, he won't bite you, he's just barking but has never bitten anyone. Welcome my friend, I'm glad you made it, and I hope you are hungry. There are a few fat Mahi-Mahi fish on the grill."

He introduced me to his friends. There were

probably around twenty people, men and women, most wearing shorts and flip flops.

They were all very welcoming and cheerful. Some of the ladies even hugged me like their lost child. On one hand, it made me feel embarrassed, but on the other hand, it made me feel like I'm part of the group, which was quite strange, considering we only met each other few minutes ago.

Jean Gler stood above the giant grill, covered with smoke. He then pulled out a few Mahi-Mahi fish that looked just perfect and ordered everybody, "Eat now. Speak later!"

In the background, I recognized the Brazilian master, Gilberto Gil, singing his covers of Bob Marley's popular songs. I felt at home and between friends.

Everybody was eating and smiling at each other. No one bothered me with the usual questions; where am I from? What do I do? Am I married?

Only after dinner, along with the coffee, they started talking. What seemed, at first, as a relaxed Hawaiian chill out party, happily ignoring the real world's problems, became an intensive debate about the global economy.

Most of these characters, who looked more like a group of aging spiritual surfers, seemed to be very posted with all the financial and geopolitical burning issues. I was totally surprised by the fact they were so knowledgeable and opinionated.

Apparently, as I learned later, they all live here in the "Traders Village". The group included financial industry veterans, Hedge Fund managers, Indie traders, and entrepreneurs, in several investment related fields.

They all arrived to Kauai, some on their own, and others with their families, in search for their own paradise, and here they found a balance between the investment world's typical stress and the easygoing lifestyle they dreamed of.

The Traders Village provided them with all the amenities and infrastructure that the modern world could offer, so they could live comfortably, trade, and communicate with the rest of the world.

It seemed they have a vivid community life. A micro universe within the island of Kauai and a micro universe within the investment world.

Jean Gler, although I'm not sure he was the older, took the role of the tribe's wise old man. Calming the discussion when it became too heated, bringing back to perception some extreme opinions, and adding an optimistic phrase to a pessimistic view, or an original Jean Gler quote.

I consider myself a knowledgeable businessman and an experienced investor, therefore, I feel quite comfortable to admit when I don't understand a term or a subject, and even ask for an explanation.

During the evening, I had many questions and heard many explanations, some of which did not at all make the subject clearer.

I found, however, comfort in the fact that I wasn't the only one. It seemed that being confused is back in fashion, as long as you can keep smiling.

The main conversation after dinner revolved around several subjects concerning the global economy, the financial industry, the investment universe, and its various segments.

To be more precise, it was all about what went wrong, what are the problems, conflicts, difficulties, etc.

LARRY & SUN

Sun is a fundamental analyst, with a "look & feel" of John Lennon. He runs his own Long/Short Equity Hedge Fund.

Larry, a bald guy covered with colorful tattoos that make his living from trading futures and options, began defaming almost everyone.

He started with the politicians, continued to the central bankers, and when he blamed the stupidity and ignorance of the people, Sun interrupted and slowed him down. "Larry my brother, why are you so negative? And how could you blame the innocent people for their ignorance?

"After all, we all agreed, more than once, that it's not just another financial crisis. It's a total financial chaos, and in chaos, everybody, even the wise and the educated, are confused, if not lost.

"I agree that some of the recent actions, taken by politicians and central bankers, were inefficient and probably even causing more damage ahead, but you know well, my friend that their job is not an easy one, and honestly, I wouldn't like to be in their place.

"We are all sitting here together in paradise. Tomorrow morning we'll be at the beach, while they will wake up to another day of war, struggling to save the world's economy, and as it appears right now, without any real success, which is even more frustrating.

"I believe that none of these policy makers has figured out how the hell we are going to come out of this deep shit situation. But I do believe in their good intentions. They are doing their best, experimenting, shooting all over, hoping that one or two bullets will hit the target, and maybe even kill one of the many evils and problems in the financial system, and we all know how many there are."

LILU

Lilu is a tall, impressive brunette, with big Almond eyes, whom Jean Gler introduced me to as his true love.

They had known each other for many years before they became a couple. Jean Gler was the portfolio manager of a top performing Global Macro Hedge Fund, and Lilu managed a Fund of Funds on behalf of pension funds and insurance companies.

During a regular quarterly update call, Jean Gler informed Lilu that he's leaving his job and about to travel, in search for his paradise on earth.

He promised to be in touch, and once he settled down in Kauai, he sent Lilu an inviting e-mail to come and visit him in paradise. She accepted the invitation, and not before long, she found herself in love with both Jean Gler and Kauai. She quit her job, moved to Kauai, and never looked back.

Along with Jean Gler, she founded the Traders Village, and here, with a few partners, she develops investment games.

Lilu served her handmade Tiramisu, which gained the guests' votes for being the best dessert ever.

She then sat down, and while keeping her relaxed posture, shared her educational view, "Well Sun, I agree about the good intentions of most people involved. I honestly do not envy any of them. They face this "mission impossible" scenario and, more or less, have the whole world expecting a miracle, or otherwise, just criticizing them.

"I have no magic solutions to offer, however, I think that they could and should win the propaganda battle by explaining properly, to the public, what the real problems are.

"A major problem of the global economy today is the overall distrust of people, of all nations, in the global financial system. They simply lost their faith in it and in its ability to recover. I believe that this time it began in what I call "The mysterious financial crisis of 2008".

"The public's inability to understand the causes and sources of any event, usually leads to their inability to understand its consequences. It's true for epidemic diseases, wars, and obviously, for a financial crisis.

"The public was told that there were a few evils to blame, for the unprecedented financial turmoil. Most of the public did not know, neither fully understood, any of the evils that usually have strange names such as Sub-Prime Mortgage Backed Securities, Collateralized Debt Obligations, and Credit Default Swaps.

"I assume that even here, around this table, where most of us have some kind of financial or investment background, not everyone is fully familiar with how the mechanism of each structure actually works."

I was listening to Lilu's speech, nodding my head in agreement. I was relieved to find out that I am a part of a public that doesn't understand.

I had to take it out and said, "Well Lilu, I'm sorry to interrupt you, but you are so right. I tried, I really tried to understand what went wrong there, but I couldn't understand all the terms and structures. It's been more than 20 years that I'm watching and reading business and financial news on a daily basis, and I manage my investments for more than 18 years.

"I read many investment books, and I believe that I gathered quite a serious amount of information about the financial markets, but I found it rather difficult to understand these complex financial instruments.

"And if I'm already in a confession mode, let me just add that quite a long time ago, I lost track of those big numbers that everyone is discussing. The US debt, internal and external, the global debt, the European one, the various rescue packages, and money printing.

"Sometimes it feels as if my brain is refusing to digest such large numbers; hundreds of billions, and trillions, and God knows what next. All these Gazillions, and still the global economy is in a mess."

My confession made everyone respond and speak at the same time, and even laugh at the incredibly large and ridiculous numbers.

Lilu said that someone has to put these numbers in order and present the total financial system's size to the public, including the global debt.

She said it's the public's right to know, and that it's crucial to understanding the problems the world is facing today.

Jean Gler, smiling, said, "There are things that we, humans, just cannot comprehend, except for some crazy genius scientists. Right there, in the library, rests in peace Stephen Hawking's book "A brief history of time". It is a fascinating read about cosmology, however, I quite lost it when it discusses the actual physical magnitude of the universe, and how tiny and insignificant we are.

"So I would say that just like we cannot grasp the size of the universe, people cannot comprehend the global debt size or the total value of the derivatives market."

BROTHER K

Brother K is a big man with a grey Afro hairstyle, a big head, and Polynesian features. He is a Professor of Anthropology at the University of Hawaii, but in the past few years, he is teaching most of his courses on-line.

He was invited to live in the village as a friend of Jean Gler. He is not a professional investor, but in recent years, he developed an addiction to on-line Forex trading.

His deep voice sounded to me like a 300 year old Baobab tree, so when he entered the conversation, everyone went silent.

BAD CREDIT GENES

He presented his theory about debt and humans' bad nature, when it comes to credit. "History shows us how lousy we are in paying our debt. Survival is inherent in our nature and so is greediness. We don't only want to eat, but we always want to eat more and consume more. We want it bigger, faster, and better.

"That's why we borrow, and that's how credit is being created, as long as we find someone that is willing to lend us. However, paying our debt is not a part of our surviving nature, and we lack the instinct and the willingness to meet our obligations.

"We forget our ideals in pursuit of earthly pleasures. We invented borrowing and then invented defaults and bankruptcies.

"We accepted the inability of individuals, companies, and governments to serve their debt, and even created legal procedures for it, so no wonder why in general, as a society, we have poor credit.

"The history of defaults is fascinating but, at the same time, truly depressing. Do any of you remember, or even better, guess, how many sovereign defaults the world has witnessed in the last 30 years? Not to mention, banks going bankrupt? Airlines? Insurers or mortgage companies?

"We all probably remember just the big stories such as Russia and Argentina, Lehman Brothers and Enron, but the full list of defaults, including the stories behind them, could easily be the subject of several thick books.

"Unfortunately, some of our friends here, who trade futures, felt the pain during the recent "MF Global" saga, and a few years earlier, with "Refco".

"For investors and traders, a collapse of a broker is one of the ultimate threats. I usually listen to you guys speaking about the "counterparty risk".

"Imagine how many people and businesses, in many different fields, are getting hurt from this systematic, unethical, and non-acceptable behavior.

"If governments have no shame, and corporates go about this way every time the going gets tough, why should individuals behave differently? Accruing a large amount of debt on your selection of credit cards, and defaulting on your mortgage doesn't carry any shame or social punishment, so maybe it's more of a social problem."

DETERIORATION OF VALUES

Sun, the "Lennon" positive character, said, "I'm a strong believer in re-education. Many people just lack the basic economic education, and they are unable to evaluate the results of their exaggerated consumption.

"On top of that, I think there is a fundamental deterioration of values, and that's where this campaign should start; educating the young generation for modesty, for consuming only what they can afford, instead of over consuming and borrowing."

Larry, the bald tattooed trader, started laughing, "Sun and Brother K, I love you both, but both of you are from a rare endangered specie that is no longer in production.

"You don't need to be a historian or a social researcher in order to understand the root of the problem. Most of us here are involved, in one way or another, in the investment world, and I assume that the recent history of bankruptcies is quite fresh in our memories.

"And regarding changing values to modesty and appropriate consumption, come on, where have you been all these years?

"We live in the "show-off" era. Hip Hop stars on MTV are showing off their dazzling jewelry and luxury cars. Popular reality shows are glorifying wealth and artificial bombastic millionaire's lifestyle.

"Both of our favorite Bobs; Dylan and Marley, probably wouldn't have gained so much popularity with the young generation of today. They both were too modest.

"Anyway, there are many more problems, and you might blame me again for being negative, and I'm sorry about it, but my friends, that's the reality we live in.

"I'd rather be negative than be a liar, and that's in general what I think about the system and the people behind the system. They are all a bunch of liars. They are fooling everyone, so a big part of our discussions today, as well as on other days, is based on false data and facts.

"And you know what? I honestly don't want to sound like one of these conspiracy fans. I don't think that the FBI killed Kennedy, and I believe that Bin Laden and Al-Qaeda were behind 9-11 and not the CIA. But still, I can hardly find one source of information that is truly reliable and transparent."

NO TRANSPARENCY

"Some countries might have better reporting procedures than others, but many times, it feels like we just live in an illusion, or simply lack the knowledge and information on how things are actually conducted.

"Some highly respected economists are continuously claiming that the Chinese authorities are tweaking and manipulating economic figures.

"For years, energy analysts have suspected that Saudi Arabia is "pumping up" its oil reserves estimations.

"It has been rumored that Greece, Portugal, Italy, Spain, as well as other countries, were continuously cheating the European Union about the real size of their debt.

"Nobody in the public knows what actually happened following Lehman Brothers' default. Most of you probably remember the intense debate we had, after we watched together "Too big to fail", the HBO drama with William Hurt as Paulson and Paul Giamatti as Bernanke. We couldn't say for sure how close the story resembled reality.

"Despite the assumption, that the US is the global advocate of "free markets", the US Treasury Office is said to be running the PPT; the Plunge Protection Team, which is responsible for protecting the stock market from a severe crash, spending fortunes for keeping the market's happy mood.

"Many times, we discussed between us the capacity and legitimacy of the "Dark Pools". While many investors believe that the negotiation and price discovery process of securities is public and transparent, and is being conducted only through the various public exchanges, some of the big market participants negotiate their biggest deals in the dark. Some major investment banks are running their own private exchanges, intermediating secretive transactions between large counterparties.

"So what do we really know? Are we informed as we think we are? According to what information should we make our investment decisions?

"As always, I suggest we should be honest with ourselves about what we don't know, and try to be as practical as we can, when we invest and trade."

While some friends already slipped to other discussions, the ones listening to Larry, seemed exhausted, and I could tell that they were nodding in agreement, just to make him stop.

EMILY

Emily was introduced to me, by Jean Gler, as the only surfer in Kauai with a double PhD (economics and computers science). She was born in Australia and lived many years in the U.S.

While completing her degrees, she was working for a couple of large financial firms, designing trading platforms, and gained a reputation for being a top trading usability expert.

Describing her lips, eyes, skin color, and perfect body, would probably take me a few hours, so I'd rather mention the one thing I didn't quite like about her appearance, and that was her short haircut.

She sat right next to me, and I thought that concentrating on what I don't like could be the only strategy to control myself and not lose my head or tongue.

Emily was smiling when she started to speak, but I could notice her tough expression. She had this kind of attitude of "Cut the bullshit".

"What's new? There is no transparency, the economy is in deep shit, and the global financial system is confronting a challenge, perhaps the toughest ever. People feel insecure and hate their banks, which deprive their savings and only care about the wealth of their principals. And I actually agree that we all have a completely wrong credit concept.

"But what are the options? Can the world's economy survive and grow with no credit? Where would we hide our money if there will be no banks?

"Most of us here in the Traders Village believe that we can change things for the better, and that our actions and inventions will eventually have a significant positive impact on the investment universe.

"We cannot cure the entire global economy, but we can contribute our part to make it better. I suggest that instead of complaining, we keep doing what we do."

Jean Gler jumped off his seat and clapped his hands, "Bravo Emily! I'm with you and also a bit tired of all these whiners.

"I think we just had enough of our usual debate, and after all, we have a new guest with us tonight that you all just met and even heard.

"I don't know him that well yet. We just met today at Poipu Beach, but he is a brave surfer. He surfed today the "Acid Drops" and survived it (some of the friends whistled and applauded), and apparently he shares some of our mutual interest in investing, so I would like to welcome brother Jorgy and raise a toast, to him and to new friendships... To Jorgy!"

THE BAND

Everyone clinked their glasses together and cheered, "To Jorgy!"

I was a bit embarrassed by this warm welcome and by the sudden attention, but it felt good, and I smiled and thanked Jean Gler, Lilu and everybody else, for their invitation and hospitality.

Jean Gler started playing with his hands and fingers like a musician with no instrument and signaled me to follow him inside the house, along with some other friends.

We entered a large room that looked like a recording studio. It was full of musical instruments; Guitars, Percussions, Saxophone, Flout, and a few other ethnic instruments such as Didgeridoo, Berimbau, and Ukulele.

Jean Gler put the Saxophone in one hand and small Bongos in the other and asked me, "Jorgy, what is your favorite instrument?"

When I replied, "I don't know", he stuck the Bongos in my hands and said, "Tonight you'll be playing the Bongos then."

Each friend chose an instrument, and we all went out again to the garden. I tried to keep up with the rhythm but played softly most of the time, not to interrupt their melodies. The others kept exchanging instruments between them, but I stuck to the bongos. We played all sorts of music; Jazz, Rock, Reggae, and of course, some Brazilian Bossa Nova.

I was especially moved, and once again, a bit embarrassed, when Brother K, with his deep voice, dedicated me the famous wandering song of Harry Nilsson "Everybody's Talkin".

I wasn't the only one moved by this song. Everybody, in this enchanted evening, was some kind of a traveler and an adventurer, and I guess this song was some kind of an anthem, so they all joined Brother K and sang the words together. I even thought I saw some tears.

It was getting late, and the friends were saying goodbye.

When I approached Jean Gler and Lilu to thank them again before leaving, Jean Gler told me, "Hey Jorgy, tomorrow is Saturday, the markets are closed, and Lilu is busy with her yoga friends. How about we go surfing together, and I will show you around the island?"

Knowing Jean Gler for almost a whole day, I already knew he's fun, kind, and caring, and so I grabbed the opportunity and responded immediately, "Sure dude, if I'm not too much of a burden on you, I will be glad and grateful."

"It will be my pleasure," he said. "I will be waiting outside your hotel, exactly where I dropped you today, at 8 AM sharp.

CHAPTER 3

POLIHALE BEACH

I felt quite full, that morning after breakfast, of food, of adventures, and thoughts. But I was still hungry for more. My knees were still hurting me and not quite cured, but I couldn't wait to be in the ocean again.

Surfing in Hawaii is what I came for, and that's exactly what I received, plus a few extra adventures, new friends, and new ideas about the economy and investments.

Out of all the economic problems of the world, I wanted to learn something for my own personal benefit. I guess that sometimes self-interest leads to wisdom.

Jean Gler was already waiting for me at the hotel parking, when I came outside. As opposed to most people I know, who take advantage of every spare minute they have to check their e-mails, read news, or play games on their Smartphones, Jean Gler was just sitting there, humming to himself.

He was smiling at me when I entered his 4-wheel truck, this time in the front sit next to him, and asked me, "Are you ready?"
"Ready for what?"

"For another day of adventures, of course, unless you are tired or still suffer from the scratches on your knees. I brought a board for you, but if you don't like it, you can take my longboard. Also, there is always snorkeling gear here, in case you want to look underwater, and sorry I didn't bring any food, there are always interesting places to eat on the way. Do you have any specific places you want to see in the island?" he asked.

"As I told you yesterday, I didn't plan this trip. It was spontaneous, and I didn't do my homework, so I honestly don't have a clue. I do know you a bit by now, though, and I trust you to show me the best places."

"Hey Brother Jorgy, you are challenging me. Of course, I know all the best places in the island; the most beautiful, the exciting ones, the highest, the coolest, the biggest waves, the best places for diving, for camping, for dancing, or just drinking beer. But obviously, there is no way we can see all that in just 1 day. I live here a little bit more than 10 years and believe me, I still explore new places."

GO WEST

"I thought we can start with the West Coast. There are plenty of surfing spots there, and I really can't imagine you suffering too much in Polihale Beach."

Having no clue about the West Coast I obviously agreed and we were on our way. I told him I had a terrific time the night before and thanked him again for inviting me.

I was quite impressed with the people I met, and naturally, was curious about their backgrounds and current activities, so I inquired about his friends and about the story of the Traders Village, and without getting into personal details, he gave me a general background on each of his friends.

I could tell that he had a warm place in his heart for each one of them.

While driving and discussing investments, he directed my attention to many points of interest; explaining about the plants, local agriculture, general history of Hawaii, and to where each turn in the road leads to.

FINANCIAL MEDIA CONSUMERS

Jean Gler inquired, "Watching you yesterday, listening and participating in the conversation, I was wondering, what is exactly your interest in investments?"

"Well," I answered without much thinking, "some people like football or baseball. Others might like Opera or Jazz. I like investments. I think of myself as an investment fan, an amateur of course, not a professional investor, but I love keeping myself abreast of the latest business news, investments, and the global markets."

Jean Gler said, "For me, and for other investment

professionals, loving investments is quite natural, but it's more than just loving it. We must know what's going on in the global economy. We must keep ourselves updated with all the relevant changes in the economy, politics, geopolitics, weather, market fundamentals and technicals, regulations etc. In many cases, we actually make our living from these changes.

"Anyway, it's encouraging that you, and many others like you that make their living from non-investment occupations, find the investment universe interesting and entertaining.

"I love my work and think it is fascinating, but more than once, I felt that people around me found it to be boring. Obviously, I was a bit offended by that. People like you change this impression, and I thank you for that. Anyway my friend," he smiled, "I am very familiar with your kind of people, "investment fans."

"Lilu and Emily call this group of people "Financial Media Consumers". This group is the subject of a continuous research they are conducting, and is the target market of several projects they work on. Without knowing it, I just caught a true living example of this specie. A wild financial media consumer," he laughed, and I started laughing with him.

"You know what"? I said, "Nobody ever called me that. I quite like the term. I think I like being a "financial media consumer", and I'm definitely a proud one."

"I am glad you are," he said. "Apparently the "financial media consumers" group is quite a big movement. Look at all these business and financial news websites and channels. It's a huge industry chasing a huge audience. Anyway, I am more curious about your personal interest. What is it that you like so much about investments?"

"Well", I said, "let me see... I love the action; the simultaneous movement of so many markets, all around the world at the same time, is fascinating. I like the stories of large profits and substantial losses, even if I have nothing to do with it personally. I like reading about legendary investors like Warren Buffet or George Soros.

"I like talking about investments. It's a social thing. Most of my close friends are interested, in one way or another, in investments. When all of us get together, whether for a Bar-B-Q, or in a bar, we always end up talking about investments. Regardless of the market we discuss, everyone has a solid view and a conviction, and often, we find ourselves voting on the critical issues of the day."

INVESTMENT NEWS

I continued, "I think that instead of wasting my time in front of the screen, watching football or reality shows, from investment news, I receive an added value. I'm becoming smarter. I expand my knowledge base. I hear different opinions of experts. All of which, increase my chances of being successful in my personal investments and becoming wealthier.

"Regarding other types of news like general news, gossip, sports etc., I tend to develop those guilt feelings. My conscious feels I am wasting my time. Yes, I enjoy myself, but I'm not being productive, which goes against the capitalistic education I've been raised on, and that's exactly why I love investment news; it gives me that great feeling of being productive."

Jean Gler was listening and seemed to be digesting what I just told him. Then he replied, "Well Jorgy, I'm glad to hear that you enjoy investment news so much. Really, it's wonderful, but I would like to tell you how I see it, as someone who is a professional money manager for more than 30 years.

"As an investor, it is definitely necessary to be posted with recent economic and business developments. However, I personally find that in many cases, the news are more distracting than helping me to make smart investment decisions.

"The incredible amount of information cannot be processed or remembered by most of us. Who, in the world, can remember so many companies' names, results, fundamentals, prices, and statistics of so many industries, sectors, and regions? Sooner or later, this huge amount of information becomes a giant salad in our heads, and no wonder we feel like throwing up.

"Because the business of investment news is about producing news, they must always produce news, even if it's irrelevant to investing. That's why we have "noisy" investment news that does not contribute to our investment decisions.

"When they run out of news, they ask for experts' opinions and recommendations. They usually interview high caliber professionals, from the entire investment spectrum, each one presenting its unique view, backed by years of experience and solid research.

"Usually, these investment gurus appear one after another, quite often providing fierce contradicting recommendations, which supposedly creates a balance, but mostly just leave the audience confused."

I was listening to Jean Gler's arguments, for and against investment news.

I consider it my favorite Hobby, and I didn't want to acknowledge that it has some disadvantages. I told him, "I see your point, but what do you suggest? Avoiding investment news?"

"No my friend," he smiled. "I personally believe that if you like and enjoy something, especially if it doesn't hurt anyone, there is no reason you should avoid it, but I think you should watch investment news through your own filters and according to your Investilosophy."

"What?" I asked. "Investi what?"

THE BUMPY ROAD

"Investilosophy," he laughed. "But you know what? Do you see this bumpy road on the left? We are taking it, and it will lead us to Polihale Beach, so let's continue our investment discussion later, and I won't forget, I owe you an explanation about Investilosophy."

As we turned left, we saw two, "not so young", ladies, carrying their backpacks and trying to hitchhike to Polihale Park.

We stopped for them, and I helped them climb the back of the truck.

They were a mother and daughter who traveled all 49 states of the USA, for the last 20 years. This time, they visited the 50th state, Hawaii. They never traveled outside the United States.

It looked as if we were driving to nowhere. The bumpy dirt road was surrounded by sugar cane plantations, and I didn't see any beach ahead of us. Since I assumed that Jean Gler knew what he was doing, I kept my mouth shut.

Jean Gler was driving slowly but in slalom like fashion. I couldn't tell if he was trying to avoid the holes or intentionally getting right into them. Anyway, he looked like he was amusing himself.

The tall dark mountains that could be seen from the road, made me feel like hiking, and I was a bit upset knowing I probably wouldn't have the time to climb them.

I had the feeling that would follow me during my entire trip to Kauai; "I have to come back!"

As we drove along that bumpy road, we entered a real desert with large sand dunes and desert plants, which I did not expect to find here. "Isn't Kauai a tropical island?" I asked Jean Gler.

And he, in return, provided me with a full

overview of the diverse topographies and climates of the various areas of Kauai.

YOU CAN FEEL THE MAH-NAH!

We arrived at the park's official entrance. We parked and walked down to the beach.

On our way, we met a friendly park ranger, wearing uniforms. He spoke in a Hawaiian accent, and he was a big local guy with a dark mustache.

I told him how impressed I was with the wild beauty of Kauai and its powerful mountains and he said, "Ya Man, you can feel the Mah-Nah", which, as he explained, is the local word for "Divine Power".

I repeated the word after him a few times and received his approval for my correct pronunciation.

We passed by a group of tourists sitting in front of their tents. They looked relaxed, happy, and out of touch from all the modern worries.

I told Jean Gler, "I'm jealous, it's been so long since the last time I slept out in a tent, and I miss it.

Then, one of the girls pulled out her Smartphone and started shouting into it. We smiled to each other, and I realized that the world has changed. For a moment, I missed those times when we had no Smartphones.

We strolled down the beach with our boards.

Jean Gler drew a map of the beach on the sand, pointing, with the branch he used for drawing, the main surfing spots, and then he pointed to the

"Queen's Pond", which if I remember correctly, is the only place for non-surfers and children to swim.

He was smiling when I mentioned I'd rather start with the beginners spot, and as we were walking there, we discussed the philosophical aspects of my surfing lesson of the previous day.

SHOWING OFF

We entered the water, and not surprisingly, Jean Gler's paddling power turned out to be stronger than mine.

He didn't wait for me and started right away to show off. He was a good surfer but not one of the best.

Although longboards are not designed for quick maneuvers, there are plenty longboard tricks, and I did see some surfers doing all kind of them, including walking on it back and forth, standing on their hands, or even taking their dog with them on the board.

But Jean Gler seemed to be very pleased with himself, just standing on his longboard and riding each wave until it faded. I noticed, however, that he never missed a wave.

He was quite systematic in catching them, and in between, he was resting, sitting on his board behind the wave's break line.

It took me a while to get into it and forget about my pain, but then it came... The free flow that makes everything else go away. It was just me, the board, and the ocean in harmony.

I was conscious, but it was as if the outer world and my thoughts were living in a parallel universe, which did not interfere with my perfect surfing planet that I was one with.

I opened my eyes under the water and above the water and said to myself again and again, "You can feel the Mah-Nah!"

Since I was surfing the shortboard, that was suitable for maneuvers, and since I forgot about my real age and shape, which I left behind on the same parallel universe, along with the outer world and my thoughts, I surpassed myself and rediscovered my long forgotten youth talent again, and just like Jean Gler, but in a different style, I started showing off.

When I was younger, my favorite maneuver was "Off the lip"; turning the board up against the wave and back down. On that day in Polihale beach, I kept doing it, again and again. It was MY "Off the lip."

Jean Gler kept cheering me every time we met behind the break line, "Hallelujah! Brother Jorgy, you're a natural born surfer."

When we rested on our boards, we discussed the different surfing styles, and he explained to me why he prefers the longboards easygoing style, and I, in turn, explained why I like the shortboard acrobatic action.

Then we exchanged boards, and I thought to myself that the longboard might be more suitable for my age, but I missed my "Off the lip".

I think that Polihale Beach has the perfect ocean conditions. It has surfing spots for many skill levels, with different heights, directions, forms, and strength of waves, and it is wild and mystical.

I think it is about a 17 miles long stretch of virgin white sand beach, and unlike many surfing spots around the world, where you see buildings or city views, in Polihale you see nothing but the desert and those dark mountains in the background.

We moved between a few spots and tried each wave until we were exhausted.

My knees began to bother me again, but I did not complain. I was too damn happy.

PIT & SWEET POTATOES

Jean Gler asked if I was hungry and without waiting for my answer, pointed to a group of hippie surfers that were sitting around a campfire on the beach.

One of them, Pit, was a friend of Jean Gler. He was a Vietnam veteran who also spent some quality time in a civil prison in the US.

After hugging each other, Jean Gler asked him, "Dude, what about food?"

Pit pointed to a big open Utah sack near the fire, "Sweet Potatoes bro. A free buffet. Eat as many as you can, and please don't bother asking me where we got it from."

Pit pulled out of the fire a generous amount of sweet potatoes, which were delicious and just at the right time. We thanked Pit and the other friends and walked back to the truck.

Jean Gler asked me, "Are you dead tired or semi tired, but curious enough for another adventure?"

I told him I was ready for another adventure, but if it could be effortless, it would be just fine.

He suggested we drive through the Waimea canyon, up until we reach the point where we could see the Na Pali Coast. "No need to walk a lot. Very little effort for a very large gain."

"I remember I saw the Na Pali Coast cliffs when I looked for info on Kauai, only few minutes before I made up my mind on coming here," I said. "They looked magical so yes, let's go. But why do we need to go through the canyon? Is it that nice?"

"Nice?" He repeated, as if the word "nice" did injustice to the place. "I never found the proper words to describe such magic and beauty; you must see it with your own eyes."

That was enough. I was sold and told him, "Let's go."

CHAPTER 4

WAIMEA CANYON

We were back on the same bumpy road. This time in the opposite direction, but still surrounded by sugar cane plantations and, again, gave a ride, in the rear cabin, to 3 "Muchileros" that came all the way from Chile.

I thought for a minute about this hitchhiking culture of Hawaii, and I thought it's a cool way to travel around and meet new people.

I thought how pity it is that probably no one would stop for you in LA or in most other places.

I knew it could be dangerous, as we've seen many times in the news. More than once, people were murdered while taking a ride or giving one.

But maybe, we just became obsessed with these horror stories, and we let them intimidate us and rob a significant part of our freedom.

Anyway, I felt like I'm in an entirely different country.

I looked at Jean Gler who was driving and humming to himself, and I thought it was quite incredible that I only met him yesterday. I felt like we were old brothers in arms.

Although he was older than me, and I already saw him as my mentor, his simple conduct, and maybe even mischief manners, made me feel that etiquette and formal courtesy were unnecessary and irrelevant.

"Coffee?" He asked.

"Sure," I said, "why not."

We entered a gas station in Waimea; the little town on the way to Waimea Canyon. Filled the tank, grabbed 2, surprisingly strong aromatic, double Espressos, and continued to the canyon.

Jean Gler mentioned that there are no gas stations in the Waimea Canyon Drive. We charged the steep Canyon drive. The road was pretty rough.

Every few minutes, Jean Gler stopped on the side of the road so we could get out and watch the continuously changing beauty.

I remembered he told me that the beauty of the canyon could not be described in words, and I told him that I was inclined to agree with him. Not so much because of the topography, but mainly because of the colors.

While height, width, depth and area, can be measured, it would be quite impossible to measure or describe the colors composition and the many tones and shades of green, brown, and red.

KALALAU LOOKOUT

We parked the truck and walked a few minutes to the Kalalau Lookout.

We stood in front of these masterpieces: The Kalalau Valley and the Na Pali cliffs.

Jean Gler, that most of the time volunteered to explain any geographical or historical detail, became quiet. He was staring at the view and seemed to be absorbing it and flowing with it.

I was quiet too, for a while, but then turned to him smiling just to ask, "Can you feel the Mah-Nah?"

"Of course I feel it, nothing but the Mah-Nah. Can you feel it?"

I felt I had to concentrate, and after a few minutes of staring at it and breathing it, I told him, "Now I can feel it. I can feel the Mah-Nah, but it's not that easy to explain. I think it looks clean or completely untouched by humans. It's a perfect example of how successful nature can be when it's left alone."

Jean Gler added in a softer voice than usual, "Maybe it's something in the air. Something we cannot actually see. For each one of us, it's something different. A unique and a personal magic.

"Also, if you look long enough, you will notice that the view keeps changing. The clouds are always moving fast here. That's why the lights and shadows are playing and creating this constant change."

We walked further and sat down on a big rock. Jean Gler suggested, "This place and these moments are an opportunity for you. Try to look at the world, your life, and who you are, from a different point of view."

I asked him what is his different point of view, and he answered, "I feel this place is blessed and full with spiritual experiences of ancient Hawaiians.

"It's not my favorite place on earth and not the most playful one. I find the beach much more enjoyable, but mountains are usually more mysterious and spiritual. The way they connect between the earth and the skies symbolizes to me other connections between opposing elements.

"The silence and their immense size create a similar effect to what I feel while staring at the ocean. It makes me feel so tiny and insignificant, and I love it."

Jean Gler stood up, raised his hands towards the sky, and closed his eyes.

I thought he was about to begin some sort of a spiritual ritual or a prayer, but then he bent down, touched the ground with his hands, and moaned, "Ouch… my back is killing me."

He was stretching for a bit longer and after a while, I asked him, "Jean Gler, do you remember the conversation we had about investments in the morning, just before we entered the bumpy road to Polihale?"

"Yes," he replied, "and I think I owe you an explanation about Investilosophy."

I told him, "If you are in a deep spiritual mood, forget about it, we can continue later."

"Well, I spend most of my days in a spiritual mood, specifically up here, where I can feel the Mah-Nah all over me, but no problem and no worries brother Jorgy, investments and spirituality go well together.

"Although many people believe that anything that is related to money is only materialistic, and it's true that the purpose of investing is actually making more money, I personally see the whole process as spiritual."

I looked at Jean Gler, standing there with his right hand raised up, like an actor in one of Shakespeare's plays, with the Kalalau Valley and the Na Pali cliffs as the setting.

I wanted to learn about investments, but now I had to listen to all his spiritual chatter. I thought about interrupting and asking him to focus on the investment side, but then I realized that his investing tips are probably a part of his, "holistic spiritual", approach, and there is no other way but "buying" it and listening to the whole package.

NEW SPIRIT

Jean Gler continued, "I used to be a materialistic guy. I believed in facts and reality, and I didn't have many doubts or questions. Then 9/11 happened.

"My office was in midtown Manhattan, so I wasn't physically hurt, but just like many other New-Yorkers, my world had been shaken. It brought up many fears and existential questions that I suddenly had to confront.

"I was managing a Hedge Fund, and I was doing extremely well financially, so I decided to take a long vacation to think about it all, and that's how I arrived in Kauai.

"I know how beautiful Kauai looks to visitors, but

living here for more than 10 years, I absorbed much more than just its beauty. It is an on going defining experience. I am the same person, but with a new spirit.

"Being here in Kauai, surrounded by the powerful nature and realizing how insignificant I am, turned me into the spiritual person that I am today.

"When the facts and reality could no longer guide me, I started to ask the obvious philosophical questions such as who are we? Where did we come from? What is the purpose of our lives?

"I read many philosophical books, but obviously didn't find any solid answers. I did find, however, some comfort when I discovered others, before me, who arrived at the same conclusions, such as "Ecclesiastes", the old and inspiring philosophical book that was written by King Solomon.

INVESTORS SHAPE THEIR REALITY

"There are various popular religions in our world and quite a few common beliefs, but some questions always remain open. Is our course of life already "written" or predetermined? Can we change our reality and future by selecting different choices?

"I quite understand people who "accept" their life and destiny and enjoy a relaxed lifestyle. However, since I arrived in Kauai, creating my unique desirable reality has become a central part of my existence.

"When people decide to control and improve their

financial destiny, they choose to be more active in shaping their reality.

"While it's true that even the best decisions, about love, health, and investments, cannot guarantee us our preferred future results, I believe that they automatically produce a great feeling and bring our reality closer to our dreams.

INVESTILOSOPHY

"A few weeks after I arrived in Kauai, I found myself missing the markets action, the decision making, and the investment universe in general. It runs in my blood and I love it, so I went back to trading. Not a full time job, just a couple of hours a day, which made me feel happy, and still does.

"I know it sounds funny, but when I watch the markets' movement, I can sometimes feel the Mah-Nah.

"So I was trading and asking myself philosophical questions, and then I realized that my approach to investing had significantly changed because of my new philosophical perspective.

"I called my new investing approach my Investilosophy. I used to be a Hedge Fund Manager, now I am an Investilosopher."

I was listening attentively to Jean Gler's story, and I actually found it both remarkable and inspiring, but when he declared himself an Investilosopher, I couldn't hold myself and started to laugh. "What? An Investilosopher? I've never heard of any Investilosopher."

Jean Gler started laughing along with me and proudly said, "I know, I am the first!"

"Is Investilosophy similar to Investment Philosophy?" I asked.

"Yes and No," he said. "Yes, because the purpose of Investment Philosophy is to define your investment approach and guidelines, and Investilosophy incorporates that purpose. And no, because Investilosophy has a much broader scope.

"Investilosophy emphasizes the personal qualities and belief system of the individual investor, over the general, unified, rules of investment philosophies such as Value Investing or Contrarian Investing, which are followed by many investors.

"Investilosophy is also the personal meeting point, for each investor, between these two separate universes; philosophy and investments."

I asked him, "Does it mean that each investor has a different Investilosophy? Should I have one?"

"Of course", he said. "Although all humans are created equal, each of us is unique; therefore, each investor's Investilosophy is also unique. Whether you have written it down or not yet, how well it is structured, focused, and effective, is another story, but you probably already have your Investilosophy."

"Well," I said, "I do have quite an investment experience, and I have learned many important investment lessons throughout the years. But honestly, I find it hard to say what my "unique" Investilosophy is."

"Your Investilosophy should reflect your life

experience and investment experience, knowledge, brain power, risk tolerance, intuition, and personality.

"Your Investilosophy may include your hold on the economy, your view of the markets: how they function, behave, and react, your perception of market transparency, and how efficient the market is.

"Your Investilosophy should also include your view of human behavior: the rational vs. irrational tendencies of humans, their reactions to threats and opportunities, their "grouping" or herd behavior etc.

"Your Investilosophy is your clear vision about your investment goals and expectations and your preferred path and pace for achieving these goals.

"You should turn to your Investilosophy whenever you encounter obstacles, distractions, difficulties, and contradicting opinions or recommendations.

"Whenever you read or watch investment news, your Investilosophy should help you distinguish between right and wrong, threat and opportunity, cheap and expensive, buy and sell, whether a trade or an investment is suitable for your portfolio.

"Investilosophy should allow you to evaluate your investments, trades, and portfolio and to determine whether you are on the right track.

"You should develop your risk management rules according to your Investilosophy."

INVESTMENT LINGO

I was trying to listen carefully to Jean Gler's

explanations. I felt that he was throwing at me too many serious and valuable principles, which I found hard to digest, so I had to interrupt him.

"Jean Gler, hold your horses. I think that I understand the overall concept and meaning of Investilosophy, and I understand that I should develop my own Investilosophy; however, it seems like there are many important details I need to take into account, and it sounds a bit complicated. Do you have any practical advice that would make it easier for me?"

Jean Gler smiled and apologized, "Sorry Jorgy, sometimes I forget myself and think that everybody is speaking my own language. I probably spend too much time with the friends of the Traders Village, and we all share the same investment lingo.

"I will try to be more user friendly, but it's not really my thing. Come on, after all I'm an Investilosopher. Does it sound like someone who is easy to understand?

"Listen, if you want practical and easier explanations, you should talk to Emily. That's her field of expertise, and her declared mission is to make life easier for investors."

"I would love to talk to her," I said. "I'm just afraid that the words won't come out. I mean you've probably noticed how gorgeous she is. Yesterday, at dinner, she sat next to me, and I couldn't find anything impressive to say to her. I also found her pretty tough, isn't she?"

Jean Gler smiled and said, "Well, she may look

tough, but I would say she's just genuine and honest. She doesn't wear any masks or play the regular socially acceptable pretending games. I do, however, agree that she's gorgeous.

"Anyway, tough or not, she could have sat wherever she wanted, and she chose to sit next to you. Maybe out of curiosity and maybe because she liked you, and if you want to find out, it's up to you.

"It's Saturday evening, and if you are not too exhausted, we can throw a campfire party on the beach, and along with all other friends, we'll invite Emily."

"Wow, that sounds like a great plan," I said. "I am tired, but who cares. I am in Kauai, and I just realized that I have a new, exciting, challenge. How about yourself Jean Gler aren't you tired?"

"A little bit, but I'm always ready to party. Plus, if there is even a slight chance that I can contribute anything to humanity and to your adventure, it's an opportunity that I shouldn't miss.

"Anyway, it's going to get cold up here in less than an hour, so let's start heading back. We can look for some firewood on the way."

We stood there for a short while, saying goodbye to that breathtaking view. I was thinking to myself that Jean Gler was right. It kept changing, and it looked somehow different from what it was when we arrived. Not only that the lights and shadows were different, but it felt like, during the time we spent there, I learned how to better appreciate this marvelous creation.

CHAPTER 5

EVENING DRIVE

We went down the Waimea Canyon Drive. Jean Gler stopped the truck a few times, and I jumped out to collect firewood until he was satisfied and said, "OK Jorgy, good work, it's enough."

The sun was setting down, and the colors of the Canyon looked darker. Before entering the highway, we stopped at the same gas station in Waimea and picked up two more of those strong espressos, to get some energy.

Jean Gler called Lilu and a few friends, telling them we were about to celebrate at the beach tonight, "We'll take care of the campfire. You can bring something to eat, and please invite only close friends." He also told Lilu "Make sure Emily is coming. Our friend Jorgy misses her, but please don't tell her that."

Jean Gler winked at me smiling, and I winked back at him, a bit embarrassed that a guy my age and in my position needs friends' help to hook up with a girl.

I was thinking about Emily, or to be exact, I was preparing myself.

I was a bit upset with myself that instead of being

spontaneous or romantic, I found myself comparing optional strategies that could potentially bring me the desired results. On the other hand, my experience taught me that business strategies could work in other fields as well.

After I summarized all the information I had about Emily, I tried to think about other relevant facts, such as the place and time we will meet and potential hazards.

Then, I had to take into consideration the limited time I had for my mission. After all, it was Saturday evening, and I was planned to fly back home on Monday afternoon.

My chosen strategy was to express my interest in her work. Most people can speak for hours about what they do, and I thought that it would be a good way to get started.

It got darker, and Jean Gler was humming to himself again. Suddenly he switched to whistling the same tune, but in a more dramatic fashion. I wasn't sure, but it was some classical tune I thought I had heard somewhere.

It sounded like he was repeating, again and again, the last part of the piece. That he either didn't want to finish it, or didn't remember how it ended.

Finally, when he did finish, I applauded, "Bravo! I think I've heard this piece before, and if I'm not mistaken, it was in a classical collection of Adagios. Do you know the name of the composer?"

"Of course," he replied, "It's Rodrigo, the Spanish composer. I fell in love with this piece, "Concierto de

Aranjuez", because of the Spanish Guitar. You should hear Paco de Lucia play it."

BACK TO INVESTMENTS

"Jean Gler, do you feel like continuing our investment discussion?" I asked him.

"An Investilosopher is always glad to speak about investments, but I suspect my friend, that your head is in another place that is even more important than investments."

"I suppose I'm more transparent than I think I am," I admitted.

"Anyway, if I keep thinking about Emily, I might get too excited. If you have the energy, I'd like to hear your opinion about investments, and I have a few practical questions."

"Go ahead Jorgy, I'm willing and able, and we have almost an hour drive ahead of us."

I continued, "Well, this time it's more about me and my personal investments. I listened yesterday to your friends' conversation about the global economy, or as they called it "the financial chaos", and you know what? It truly feels great to be a part of the confused majority, but I still have no idea what should I do next, or change in my investments.

"I actually like the idea of Investilosophy, and I think I'm going to develop one of my own, but it seems like an ongoing effort for the long run. What about right now? Or next week? Is there anything urgent I should do? I don't know if it's our investment conversations of the past two days, or maybe your suggestion to look at things from a different point of view when we stood there in the Kalalau Lookout, but I feel that my perception is starting to change."

"I'm very glad to hear that," he seemed pleased. "I guess you are growing. It will be my pleasure to discuss your personal investments, but before that, I'd like to give you a proper disclaimer about risk which applies to all investors. Can I assume that you are familiar with "Disclaimers"?" he asked.

"If you mean the long text that nobody reads and that needs to be approved when you open a brokerage account, the answer is yes," I said.

Jean Gler continued, "There are many types of disclaimers, but I guess you're right, the one thing all disclaimers have in common, other than describing the risk involved, is that most investors never read them. Unfortunately, disclaimers do a better job covering brokers and regulators' asses than bringing this imperative information to the attention of clients. Anyway, let's talk a bit about risk.

RISK MANAGEMENT

"I think that the majority of individual investors neglect the most important part of investing, which is risk management. Many investors like to talk about it, but very few actually manage their portfolio risk.

"When you invest your money, with the aim of

making money, you must always be prepared for the other option, which is losing money. You must be fully aware of how much you can lose.

"Risk management is a broad subject. To begin with, I would suggest 3 basic questions you need to ask yourself: How do you define risk? How do you measure risk? How do you manage risk?

"For example, you can define risk simply as a market movement in the opposite direction of your positions. You can measure it by the percentage of portfolio loss, and you can manage risk by limiting your losses, either on individual positions or on your entire portfolio.

"This is just the beginning. You should always continue to develop and refine your risk management.

"Other than investment risk, there are several other types of risks, and believe me Jorgy, I'm not trying to frighten you just for fun or complicate things for you.

"Thinking of the unthinkable and constantly searching for threats is part of my routine as an investor. Being paranoid is quite tiring but can save your ass when things go out of control.

"I will just share with you briefly, then, some of the items that are on my regular "Paranoia List". I personally recommend that instead of being a passive paranoid, you become an active one, but it's up to you if you want to prepare and take actions in order to protect your money and yourself.

"There is always a possibility that your bank or broker goes bust. It really doesn't matter how large and respected they are, or how many centuries they are in business. As I see it, everyone is a suspect so don't put all your eggs in one basket.

"I know that splitting your savings and investments between a few accounts can give you a headache, but, on the other hand, it might save you from a heart attack when things go wrong.

"A few other threats with different consequences, are hyperinflation, deflation, and if we think big enough, depression and sovereign defaults. To finish this short "Paranoia List" I'd like to cheer you up with some of my favorite extreme threats, as food for thought.

"Natural disasters like hurricanes, floods, earthquakes, and tsunamis. Not so natural, but still disastrous, are wars; regional, world, biological, chemical, and nuclear wars. And if we move on to "science fiction", we can find plenty of inspiring threats like an enormous meteor hitting earth or aliens attacking us.

"I obviously hope that all those threats will forever remain in my "Paranoia List" as theoretical threats only, but if they don't, at least you won't be able to complain that I didn't warn you.

"And now let's talk about your investments. If you want some practical recommendations, tell me a bit about your current investments, and try to be specific in your questions."

While Jean Gler swiftly changed the subject, I was dwelling on those threats "What's the point?" I asked him. "If we'll die anyway, sooner or later, from a tsunami, nuclear war, or a meteor, why should we bother?"

Jean Gler seemed amused, "Sorry Jorgy, I didn't mean to put an extra load on your shoulders, but as you know, living is a risky business. Anyway, let's get back to your investments."

I thought for a moment and began describing my investments, "OK…I'm quite a conservative investor. I only invest in Stocks and bonds, either directly or through Mutual Funds and ETFs. Approximately 50% in Stocks and 50% in Bonds. My Portfolio is diversified with different stock sectors, some foreign stocks and various bonds maturities, mostly sovereign but also corporate.

"Do you think it is the right balance for the current market environment or for the financial chaos we live in?"

"No, I don't," he answered assertively.

"Why not?"

He took a short break and sighed, "Well Jorgy, I gave you the short answer, but the explanation is quite long, and I'm just trying to be user-friendly, or less complicated in my explanation. I must admit, though, that it doesn't come naturally to me, so I'm trying to find the right words to deliver my message to you, but before I start, do you have more questions?"

"Well," I said, "I obviously want to hear why not, but if that's not the right balance, what is then? Do you think that non-professional investors can make profits on their investments in this financial chaos?

"What is the best strategy for such times of uncertainty?

"Do you think that I should change my investment approach?

"And if you don't mind me asking, what do you, Jean Gler, invest in?"

Jean Gler straightened himself up in his seat, "All right Jorgy, now you're talking. I will do my best and maybe even kill a few birds with one stone, before we get to the beach.

"You have to understand that all my investment recommendations are derived from MY Investilosophy, while you should make investment decisions according to YOUR Investilosophy, and I think I already said enough about Investilosophy today.

"As you can imagine, there is no one definite answer to most investment questions, because no one knows the future and there are so many opinions. It would be quite interesting if you present the same investment questions to our friends around the campfire."

I smiled and told him, "It would definitely be interesting, but I don't want to be the cause of another argument between Larry and Sun. Plus, like you mentioned this morning regarding the investment recommendations, too many opinions might just confuse me. Right now, I'm interested in your opinion and arguments. What's wrong with my portfolio? And please save me all the disclaimers."

"OK Jorgy, but before I continue, let me just ask you 2 more questions. Are all your investments long only?

"Do you, or any of the funds that you invest with,

invest in other asset classes other than stocks and bonds?"

Since I was familiar with the terms long and short, buy and sell, and since I read about certain funds that utilize various investment strategies or that invest in other asset classes, I answered him, "As far as I know, my entire portfolio is long only stocks and bonds."

TRADITIONAL & ALTERNATIVE INVESTMENTS

Jean Gler began explaining, "Stocks and Bonds are considered "Traditional Investments", as long as you don't sell them short or utilize other "Alternative" strategies when trading them. You probably heard the term "Alternative Investments" which includes various strategies and asset classes with different characteristics, legal structures, and liquidity terms."

"Yes I did," I said, "I am familiar with hedge funds, private equity, and venture capital."

"Good Boy Jorgy, I'm glad you've done your homework," he continued. "Just so you have a general idea of where in the investment universe I'm coming from, I will mention that I'm considered a Global Macro investor, and it can be categorized under hedge fund strategies. Without getting into details about my current positions, in general, I trade both sides, long and short, several asset classes such as equities, commodities, and currencies.

"I say trade and not invest, not because I do it frequently, but just to differentiate it from the common "buy and hold" practice. Although some of my trades have longer holding periods, I never hold any asset for the long run just out of a blind faith that it must go up.

"When I say equities, I mean stocks, but I never trade individual stocks, only stock indices. Instead of following thousands of companies, I look at the entire stock market, just as another asset that I can either long or short.

"In my view, and please excuse me as I have no intention of hurting your feelings, "Traditional Investments", as well as your investment strategy are part of the previous century.

"Investing passively in stocks and bonds is, in my opinion, nothing but irresponsible, and believe me, I'm trying to be gentle with you.

"By investing passively I mean that probably the only action taken, in any possible scenario, is fine-tuning the balance between stocks and bonds, and increase or decrease your cash.

"It doesn't matter if we call the current situation deep shit, a financial chaos, uncertainty, or faltering growth. It really doesn't matter. What matters is how your portfolio will react and perform in any possible market scenario.

"You are a financial media consumer after all. I'm sure you are familiar with some of the doom's day prophecies that are either predicting a severe market crash or a continuous bear market.

"Although I hope for better scenarios, I cannot entirely eliminate the worst case scenarios. How will your portfolio of 50/50 stocks and bonds perform in such scenarios?

"Are you willing or able to absorb significant losses? What actions will you take if your worst case scenario happens?

"You claim that you are a conservative investor, that you invest in stocks and bonds, and that your portfolio is diversified. Now let's separate the discussion to stocks, bonds, diversified, and conservative, and let's try to discuss each of them separately.

"Investing traditionally in stocks, and as always, I'm not sure if my descriptions are similar to investment dictionary definitions, involves the purchase of stocks with the hope that they will appreciate in price, and then you, the investor, will make a profit.

"There are numerous stock strategies, many more than any of us can remember. Long only stock strategies are based on the assumption that, for whatever reason, the price of the stocks you purchased will increase.

A DIRECTIONAL BET

"While each stock's price can go up, down, or sideways, these stock strategies are only successful if the price goes up, or in other words, they are all based on a directional bet.

"Basing your investment strategy on one directional bet is, in my view, irresponsible, and maybe even dangerous in times of a financial chaos.

"Jorgy, since you are an experienced investor, I don't think I need to elaborate on the consequences of a wrong directional bet.

"Now, before we go over to bonds, let's talk briefly about your stocks diversification, unless you want to ask something or if you feel it's too much or too fast."

"No," I said, "go on, I'm in a bit of a shock, but it's interesting, and I actually like your speed, it's probably that double espresso... But please go on, I will stop you if I'm confused."

"So, diversification," he said, and was about to continue when I stopped him, "Just a minute, you know what, I would actually be glad to hear what can I do or should do, instead of basing my investment on a bet?"

LEARN TO SELL SHORT

"On a directional bet, you mean," he corrected me and continued. "The answer is that first, you have to be able to bet on both directions, up and down. Today we will leave the 3rd direction which is sideways, out. You probably heard of strategies that can benefit from it.

"In order to profit from a down market movement, or from a continuous bear market, you want to sell short. Are you familiar with the term? Did you ever short any security?"

"Yes," I answered, "I am familiar with the term and how it works, but no, I never sold short, I'm not sure why. I guess that short selling is somewhat

72

counterintuitive. I read many investment books, and I learned that eventually stocks outperform any other asset class, even after a market crash, and despite some bear markets in history, so I find it hard to go short. Also, it always sounds like an illogical action, selling something you don't even own."

"It's all right Jorgy, I do understand your reasoning, but let me respond to both issues you raised. I assume that those books, which claim that stocks will always eventually go up, probably base their arguments on past performance, more likely the previous century's performance.

"Please don't get me wrong. Personally, I'm an optimist who believes it's not the end of the world, and it is in the best interest of too many powerful entities that the global economy will get back on track, and that the stock market will rally.

"But what if it doesn't?

"Can we be sure that the stock market will perform in this century as it performed in the last century? My honest answer is that I don't know, and I'd like to be ready to profit in various possible scenarios.

"Regarding your reluctance to go short, you are not alone. It is a very common psychological barrier for many investors and actually, Lilu's company developed an investment game that is designed to remove this common barrier."

"Really?" I asked. "Do you think I am suffering from a psychological barrier to go short?"

"Of course," he replied, "but no worries, Lilu

found the cure for it and it's an easy game. Once you manage to climb to the highest level, you win the game, and you are up and ready to go short with confidence. Now let's talk about diversification."

DIVERSIFICATION

"I never made any official survey, neither read about it anywhere, but if I have to throw a wild guess, I'd say that it's one of the most popular words in the investment universe, if not THE word. Unfortunately, too many people believe that diversification is the best way to manage risk.

"While diversification has various advantages, it doesn't replace a well structured risk management framework. Diversification can prevent losses only when you diversify with non-correlated assets.

"Diversifying a stocks portfolio with more stocks, with the hope it will prevent losses in a market crash, is ridiculous. All stocks correlate. Large, Medium, and small Cap. Value, Momentum, or Growth. Banking, Energy, Technology, and all other sectors. US, Europe, Asia, or Emerging Markets.

"Sometimes one group outperforms the other, and on another day or year it's the opposite, but as I see it, they all correlate.

"You know what, I do know a few smart people that are consistently making money by predicting which sector or region will outperform the other, but as I said, there are only few of them.

"If you take all stocks and categorize them by sector or size, you will see slight differences in performance on a daily basis, but when the going gets tough, the tough don't get going, they go down! When the market crashes, all stocks crash together.

"What can you do about it? You can and should diversify with other asset classes that are not correlated to stocks, and I don't mean bonds. We'll get to bonds in a minute.

"By "not correlated" I mean, either assets that react differently than stocks to similar economic environments and events, or assets that their price is influenced by different factors than stocks.

"You should always be on the guard and verify that the non-correlation continues. If it changes and your various diversifying assets begin to correlate, you should look for other non-correlated assets."

Jean Gler was speaking louder and faster than usual, but I liked his determination and conviction. I stopped him and asked, "Jean Gler, do you have any good examples for non-correlated assets?"

He replied, "Look Jorgy, there are tons of them out there, but the problem is that in times of chaos, the correlations between assets can change abruptly. It is the subject of continuous academic researches, and I believe that understanding the reasons behind those changes is essential to producing non-correlated returns.

"I will be glad to give you many fascinating examples from the commodities markets, but because I love commodities so much, when I start talking about it, it's hard to stop me, so I suggest we first talk about your bonds, and if we have time, we'll get back to commodities stories. OK?"

"OK," I agreed, "let's talk about bonds, but I'm now curious about commodities."

"If you are that curious," Jean Gler said, "I can give you a great exercise. Go to any commodities website that provides historical long-term charts. Looking at how commodities behaved in the past 5 to 20 years can give you a good idea about the times they did not correlate with stocks or with other commodities.

"The following exercise would be to find out why. What were the reasons behind the non-correlation? In what environment stocks went up and commodities went down? Which commodities went up in a bear stock market?"

"Oops, there I go again..." he said, "I told you that speaking shortly about commodities is not an easy task for me."

"Yes, I can see," I replied, "but it's interesting. Just tell me, please, on what commodities I should concentrate."

Jean Gler sighed, "Look Jorgy, there are more commodities than I can remember, but to begin with, you can look at some of the most commonly traded commodities such as Gold, Oil, Copper, Wheat, and because we already drank a couple of cups today, add Coffee to the list.

"I promise you that behind each commodity's chart there are fascinating stories and lessons about history, economy, politics, geopolitics, climate patterns, and human behavior. I'm not being objective, but I'm pretty sure you will find commodities a fascinating subject. Now let's speak about bonds," Jean Gler continued. "Do you want the short version or the long reasoning behind it? And I warn you, it's heavy stuff."

"Well, first the short version and then the long reasoning."

STOP INVESTING IN BONDS

"Fine then. In short, you should stop investing in bonds!"

"What?" I looked at him surprised. "The safest and most conservative investment... The core of any institutional respected portfolio... Why should I stop investing in Bonds?"

"Tell me Jorgy, can you still feel the winds of change of the Kalalau Lookout?"

"Well," I told him, "up until now, most of what you've said made sense, so of course I'm open to new ideas, please go on."

He continued, "I am aware of the consensus around bonds. Indeed, they are considered a safe haven, and represent a significant part of many respected institutional portfolios, and I do realize that there are many investment experts that would harshly criticize my recommendation. However, I'm not the first one who says, "Hey look, the Emperor is naked!"

"Only yesterday, we were listening to Brother K's theory about the bad nature of humans when it comes to credit and the long history of defaults, both sovereign and corporate. Come on, look around, it happened many times in history, and it's happening now.

"Would you consider lending money to a friend that already owes large amounts of money to others? I'm not hinting in any way that we, the U.S of A, or any other developed country will default anytime soon, but it is always a possibility.

"My intention is to shed some light on how ridiculous the phenomenon is; the common people are risking their savings by lending to the mighty empires, for just a fraction of an interest rate.

"You know what? When bonds offer such ridiculous rates, I don't consider them eligible investments.

"I know that most investors will keep investing in bonds even if there is an increased risk of sovereign or corporate defaults, and even if the interest rate they are promised to receive is zero or negative.

"But I believe there is nothing wrong in questioning, from time to time, what stands behind our beliefs and habits, and right now, I believe that investing in bonds is a very bad habit.

"The ones that are claiming there are no other alternatives are closed minded. For individuals who are nimble and creative, there are always alternatives.

MANAGE STRESS & INFORMATION

"Now Jorgy, let me ask you that, do you still consider yourself a conservative investor?"

"Honestly," I responded, "I really don't know. I guess I will have to think about it, but you brought to my attention some very interesting points, thank you."

"You are most welcome, it is my pleasure," he said and continued. "Just to summarize and to answer your other questions. Yes, I think that non-professional investors can and should profit in this chaotic environment.

"There isn't one single winning investment strategy to trade these markets. You should invest according to your own Investilosophy. And yes, I would definitely encourage you to change your approach to investing."

"Thank you Jean Gler, I appreciate your honesty. Is there any other advice I should take back home with me?"

He thought for a while and said, "Well Jorgy, I'm trying to give you my best advice, but I'm afraid I've already overloaded you with TMI. "Too Much Information" is a major problem for investors, especially in the internet era, and we already talked about investment news in the morning.

"I suggest you learn how to manage and limit the amount of information you process on a daily basis. If you limit your investment themes to anything between 4 and 10, you will obviously need to digest a smaller amount of information, and you will be able to become an expert in your selected investment themes.

"My final recommendation to you is learn to manage stress. If you have any kind of stress, at work, relationship, traffic, etc., you should find ways to reduce and control it. Yoga is the favorite pick nowadays, but surfing, dancing, or any other activity that reduces stress, is equally good. Calm investors achieve better results.

"Anyway, we'll be at the beach in 3 minutes. I don't know when everybody else is about to arrive, but I do want to wish you good luck in your romantic endeavors. We had a long day my friend, but the night is young."

CHAPTER 6

THE CAMPFIRE

We arrived at the beach at the foot of the Traders Village. I helped Jean Gler unload the firewood, and together we arranged them in a cone shape. Jean Gler took out of the truck a gigantic raffia rug, and I helped him place it a bit further from the firewood.

He lay down, looked around, and then said, "Jorgy, I think we've done our part, now the others should take care of all other arrangements, and I specifically mean food. They will probably arrive soon so in the meantime, we have a chance to rest a bit or take a nap."

My mind was full of thoughts about adventures, investments, and most of all, about Emily, so I couldn't sleep, but I did position myself in the optimal resting position on the raffia rug. And then the mosquitoes came.

MOSQUITOLOSOPHY

My attempts to drive them away weren't successful.

They were attacking me with no mercy, as if they

were starving for days before they found me and were now celebrating the successful hunt.

Jean Gler, who was already sleeping for a while, woke up from the noise I made, fighting the mosquitoes. He opened his eyes, fresh as if he slept a whole night and said, "Good morning Jorgy, I see that you have new friends."

I already noticed that Jean Gler had something to say about most things, so obviously he had something to say about mosquitoes as well. He sat down and began another lecture. "Look Jorgy, the mosquitoes represent a great lesson. Why did God, or whatever it is that you believe in, created such annoying creatures that are useless, only bite, and make us suffer?

"Our inability to understand the reasoning behind the existence of mosquitoes shows us again how little we know. We do know, however, that there are nasty creatures everywhere. They may take the form of animals or humans, and they get on our nerves.

"I intentionally refrain from saying that mosquitoes are evil, because I don't know whether they have intentions or feelings, although many times I swore I saw the devil in each one of them.

"Here in Kauai, they definitely disturb our hippie "I am in a Nirvana" mode, but they cannot take away our high spirits, nor our desire and willingness to spend some quality time close to Mother Nature. We can live a peaceful life despite them.

"Ask people "How does Heaven or Paradise look like?" And I bet the majority will say, "Turquoise water, white sand beaches, and palm trees". All these heavenly places are governed by mosquitoes.

"But don't worry too much. I'm sure some of our friends have insect repellent, probably even an organic one. Everything is organic today, and green, and anti-aging, and prevents cancer. They should be here any minute now."

Obviously, I was playing the cool guy next to Jean Gler. Unfortunately, it's not socially acceptable to be hysteric, but until the others came, the mosquitoes had bitten each and every part of me. I thought I was going mad.

People usually say that, in the end, we forget our bad experiences and remain with the good memories. Well, this time I suppose, it will take me longer than usual...

Trying to keep myself busy, I decided to light the campfire. I asked Jean Gler for the matches and thought that by moving around, I will confuse the mosquitoes, but I was dead wrong. Apparently, they loved a good challenge.

NO WOMAN NO CRY

Jean Gler looked at me as if he had a sudden revelation. "I'm sure you know Bob Marley's song "No woman no cry", right?"

"Of course I know this song, who doesn't?" I replied.

"Then you should know what is so exciting in this very moment right here."

"Is it anything to do with mosquitoes?" I asked.

"No," he was disappointed. "Come on, think about it. What's your name? And what is it that you are doing right now?"

I guess I was so obsessed with the mosquitoes' bites, it was all I could think about.

Jean Gler could not wait any longer and solved the riddle for me. "Your name is Jorgy. You are lighting the fire. And Bob Marley sings..." and Jean Gler started to sing while moving his head to the rhythm,

"...I remember when we used to sit
In the government yard in Trench Town
And Jorgy would make the fire lights
Logwood burning through the nights..."

I finally got it. I managed to squeeze a smile and tried, with little success, to pretend I'm excited.

THE FEAST

Then the friends started arriving. I tried to be polite, but wasn't that nice or relaxed until someone gave me a repellent. It took me a while to get over it, then the itching calmed down and the mosquitoes stopped biting me.

I already knew some of the friends, but some were new to me. They all brought with them an impressive amount of food and drinks, blankets, and of course, guitars and other musical instruments.

Just one thing was missing, the only thing I cared about and the reason for all this gathering. Emily.

I took Jean Gler aside for a moment and whispered impatiently in his ear "Where is Emily?"

He told me, "wait a minute, I'll ask Lilu."

"No," I said anxiously, "forget about it, I don't want to make it an issue."

"Why not? Isn't she THE issue of this campfire?" He asked, and without waiting for my answer, he went to exchange a few words with Lilu. When he came back, he said, "No worries my friend, she'll be here, but she had a prior dinner commitment with friends in Lihue. She promised Lilu to dodge as soon as she can and join us at the campfire, so just relax and be patient, and try to have some fun."

Brother K approached us, and while handing us recycled paper cups and filling them with wine, he said, "Jorgy and Jean Gler, you both look so dry, you must try this wine. It's an exquisite Chardonnay, and it is produced in Maui on the slopes of the volcano Haleakala."

I don't know if it was that good, or if I needed it so badly, but I drank the entire cup in one go.

Brother K was pleased and said smiling, "I see you like it very much, so let's finish this bottle; I brought a full case of them." Throughout the night, he was obsessed with filling everyone's cups.

Everyone came hungry, so it took only a short while for the feast to begin. The campfire was already burning for a while, and Jean Gler pulled some burning coals out of it and filled the grills. Within a few minutes, the whole area smelled of grilled fish and Lobsters.

We then pulled out of the fire the potatoes, taro, and other roots I didn't recognize. We were all busy eating, drinking, or as they called it, "sharing".

Some of the friends were talking about the recent revolutions around the world, how it will be recorded in the pages of history, and the impact it will have on us.

Then somehow, they went back to the previous evening's discussion about the financial chaos we live in, and just like the previous evening, Sun and Larry presented opposing opinions.

They were both worried. Sun was worried because of the deflationary pressures and Larry, on the other hand, claimed that hyperinflation is a sure thing to come.

INVESTMENT GAMES

While they were still arguing, Lilu, who seemed a bit tired of this never ending debate, turned to me and asked, "Jorgy, I understand you had a long day. How do you find Kauai so far?"

"I'm in love," I declared. "It is much more beautiful than I could have ever imagined. You are very fortunate to live on such an amazing island. We had a glorious day. We surfed in Polihale, we drove through the Waimea canyon up to the Kalalau Lookout, and Jean Gler kept entertaining me and told me all about his Investilosophy."

"Poor guy," she said smiling. "Did he blow your mind?"

"A little bit," I answered, "but he also gave me some very practical recommendations about my investments, and apparently, I'm suffering from the common psychological barrier that is deterring me from selling short."

"Welcome to the club," she greeted me humorously.

"Jean Gler told me you invented a game that's supposed to solve this problem."

"Yes, me and my team," she said. "It's fun and simple, and after a few days of playing, most users forget their inherent fear of selling short."

"Does your company develop other games?" I asked.

"Of course," she replied, "we have an entire line of investment games. Each game has its own purpose. Some games are just pure fun and are designed to visualize the exciting trading action, while other games are educational, where the users gradually progress to higher game levels, according to their investment achievements.

"We develop investment games for both experienced investors like you, and also for beginners. The design and interface can be customized for different demographic groups such as young mothers, pensioners, and teenagers.

"As you have probably noticed already Jorgy, most of us here in the Traders Village live and breathe investments. Thanks to our personal enriching and enjoyable experience with investments, we believe that apart from the profit potential, investing is challenging and therefore, a healthy activity that helps develop, maintain, and improve brain functions.

"Many people refrain from investing because they perceive it as complicated and boring. It is easier to attract people to play games than trying to convince them to invest."

I was quite impressed with Lilu's answer and said, "I must admit that it sounds very interesting, and you make a convincing argument about the link between investments and brain functions. I will obviously be glad to play your investment games, and who knows, I may even get rid of some psychological barriers."

"I'm sure you will," she smiled.

I was quite curious about her personal story and felt comfortable enough to ask her. "I understand that you had a long and successful career, managing an institutional Fund of Hedge Funds, before you came to Kauai so why did you leave the Hedge Fund business, and how did you come to develop investment games?"

She replied, "I left because I found Jean Gler and Kauai, and because I was a bit tired of doing the same thing for such a long time.

"Since the beginning of my career, I was a part of the investment universe. I always loved it but there were too many things that bothered me, and I wanted to do something about it.

"I wanted to change the old investment universe, to stir it up, and to enrich it, so I decided to channel both my passion and frustration to promoting the vision I had in mind.

"The investment games we develop are just one segment of the total investment vision that we all share.

"The world around us is changing, and it's changing fast. We haven't said a word, and suddenly everything became social. We turned our heads away for another second, and now it's all mobile. Just look at the music and film industries as examples, where the business models have changed entirely.

"My point is that for whatever reason, social or technological, the world has moved forward, and the investment industry, in my opinion, is still lagging behind.

"Instead of blaming governments, regulators, banks, brokers, or the innocent public again, I prefer contributing my part.

"I believe that human creativity has no limits, but we haven't yet seen the beautiful side of it flourishing in the investment universe. Although lately I do see more and more innovative applications, I think it is just the beginning.

"Basically, instead of concentrating my efforts on producing non-correlated returns for my clients, I decided to focus on new ideas that will create an attractive, enjoyable, and healthy investment universe."

"Lilu, I wish you the best of luck, it sounds fantastic," I said, "but do you truly believe that you alone can change the entire investment industry? And while you are here in Kauai?"

"Of course, why not," she replied. "First, I'm not

alone. We have a team of talented people from different fields, including finance and investments, gaming, programming, design, and marketing.

"Regarding our location, I don't think that, in today's web based world, it is an obstacle. I mostly see the advantages of being here in Kauai. We are not distracted by the competition and the financial world hype. We have plenty of time and the peace of mind to come up with, and develop, exciting new ideas."

Jean Gler who approached Lilu to hug her, heard us speaking and added in his half joking half serious tone, "Well Jorgy, think about David and Goliath. Lilu is obviously like David, and I will not be surprised if she kills a few giants on her way."

And Lilu said, "Although I have a lot to say about financial giants, I really don't think I would have to kill any of them. It's either they adapt to the culture of innovation and creativity, or they cease to exist."

GAMBLERS VS. INVESTORS

Brother K, who approached us to fill our recycled cups with his exquisite Maui Chardonnay, interrupted, "talking about me? Did I hear the word giants?"

Lilu, amused by him answered, "No worries Brother K, you are a giant, but one with a giant heart, so I think we'll let you live. We were talking about investment games, not giants."

Brother K was flattered, "Thank you dear. You

know I love your investment games, but what about the Forex game you promised me? The one that will help me lose less."

"I promise you, it's on our list big guy. It's just that we have prior commitments, but we already have the concept and game design document."

"What kind of a game that would be?" I asked Lilu.

And she responded with a question, "Are you familiar with foreign currency markets and the various On-line Forex trading platforms?"

"Of course," I answered, "I have a bunch of friends playing those games, but since they usually lose money, I always thought it wasn't for me."

"OK," she said, "but just to make it clear, these are not games, but real time trading, of real world markets. I know that because of the action and speed, they are sometimes mistaken for games.

"Anyway, this particular game is designed to teach Forex traders how to manage the overall risk of their portfolio. However, I admit that I'm a bit skeptic about the ability of Forex traders to develop self-discipline. Brother K, by the way, is our inspiration, and this is one of the reasons I'm skeptic."

"Thank you again dear," said Brother K.

"You are most welcome darling," Lilu laughed and continued. "While I do know some professional money managers that are able to consistently produce high risk adjusted returns in the Forex markets, it's quite a consensus that the majority of individual investors are losing money on those on-line platforms.

"Whether Forex trading is pure gambling or a skill that combines analysis and risk management, it seems like this group of Forex traders doesn't really care. They are mostly doing it for fun."

Brother K looked at Lilu, took a deep breath, and began another one of his theatrical speeches, "My dear Lilu, you hit the nail on the head. Indeed, I do it for fun, but obviously, I never lose hope of becoming much wealthier in a matter of days, or maybe even hours.

"What is so appealing about being rich? Is it the money itself? The glamour? Or the things it can buy?

"Why do we all, except for the Dalai Lama, want to be wealthier?

"Isn't it, this one trait that unites us, humans, to a one big group that shares the same fantasy?

"And maybe it is exactly this hope that both gambling and investment shops are selling us?

"What are the differences between investing and gambling?

"What characteristics do investors and gamblers have in common?

"Which group is larger?

"How many investors are also gamblers? Etc. Etc. Etc...

"I have no statistics to report my friends, but I would say that it could be an interesting subject for an academic research. The thesis might argue that investors are left-brain people, logical, and analytical, while gamblers are right-brain people, intuitive, and emotional.

"As far as I'm concerned, I admit that I tend to have some gambling addictive characteristics in my personality, however, I prefer Forex trading to on-line Casinos, because trading gives me the feeling that I have an edge, or am becoming smarter, which is absolutely an illusion, of course.

"My experience and knowledge do improve my predicting abilities at times, but other times, they don't. One thing for sure is that risk management is a skill that can be learned, practiced, and improved with time, and I'm pleased to inform you, my dear friends that, nowadays, I'm losing a lot less."

We were all pretty amused by Brother K's speech and started discussing the investors vs. gamblers issue.

Suddenly I heard a familiar voice, accompanied by another non-familiar voice with a Latin accent. Both were women's voices.

"Hi everybody... Hi everybody."

I recognized Emily's voice, and there she was. Hugging and kissing everybody. I wasn't really jealous, just a bit annoyed that I had to wait so long for my turn.

Wasn't it my "event"? After all, this beach party was planned and arranged just for my personal benefit. My turn finally arrived.

This hugging habit, which just the night before seemed to me as old-fashioned and an unnecessary burden, now appeared to me as my only salvation.

"Emily, what a surprise!" I said and hugged her.

It was a close hug, and fragrant, and warm, and

very long. I gathered all my mental strength, and I finally let go.

CAMILA

I stared at Emily and compared my fantasies to the fabulous reality that stood there, right in front of me. I obviously looked at her in a different light than the night before, and I don't mean the campfire's light. She was gorgeous and a bit softer than the night before.

"Wait a minute," she said, "I want you to meet my best friend. Hey Camila, come say hello to Jorgy." So she came.

Shining, smiling, fresh, and too damn sexy. Right into my arms, to the traditional hug.

I think I was in a brief shock or some sort of confusion. I forgot the words and strategies and just stood there smiling, maybe like a child, probably like an idiot. I am not sure.

It was Brother K that came to my rescue, with his deep voice and exquisite Chardonnay, "Ladies, can I offer you some white wine? And you Jorgy, you look so thirsty."

He filled our cups, and we all sat down together near the campfire that was already much smaller by now.

Camila was born in Argentina and arrived to New York to pursue her interdisciplinary career. She was a programmer, a designer, and an animator.

During a branding project for a large financial firm, she met Emily and they became friends. She wasn't a surfer, but when Emily suggested she joined her on a trip to Hawaii, she thought it would be nice to get out of the city for a while.

On their way back from Kauai's North Shore, Sun gave them a ride, and when he mentioned he was managing a Hedge Fund out of the Traders Village, they became curious, so he brought them for a visit, and the rest is history.

Camila and Emily share a large house in the Traders Village, and together they run the "Investilizer", a company that develops user-friendly trading platforms.

While Emily had that short haircut that bothered me and kept me focused, and she was a bit tough, Camila seemed to lack such features.

She looked too good to be true. She was so nice and so sweet, and on top of that, she had this Spanish accent that truly drove me crazy.

I'm actually holding myself right now, when writing, not to explicitly describe her sensual figure, and not to repeat every word she was saying with this lovely seducing pronunciation.

I was sitting there, with these two lovely girls, telling myself what I've been taught, "Stick to the plan. Turn on your charm. Be persistent."

So I did. I expressed my interest in Emily's business, but then it turned to be their business, and they both seemed to be so happy to "share it" with me.

Just when I decided that the right thing to do is to concentrate on Emily and forget about Camila's beauty and cuteness, Camila placed her hand on my knee and asked, "Hey Jorgy, what are you doing tomorrow?"

I almost choked, thinking she's coming on to me and even worse, stealing me from her friend and partner, Emily. I started murmuring something like, "Eh...ah...I...I don't know."

She continued, probably thinking I'm too drunk or tired, or maybe realizing that I'm embarrassed, "Listen Jorgy, we are going to the North Shore tomorrow, so if you don't have other plans, you can come with us."

I didn't know what to say. "Who are WE? Wait a minute; it's not according to the plan. I should be wooing Emily right now. Hey Jorgy, wake up, be focused."

Then Emily said, "Come on Camila, let's be honest here. Even if he does have other plans, do you actually believe there's anything that can compare to us?"

Now I was totally confused, and my thoughts ran in different directions simultaneously. "Is this what I think it is? If it looks like... and smells like... it probably is... but what if it's not? What if one of them wants me and the other doesn't? What if it's just the opposite? What if they are both interested? And what if I'm just hallucinating?"

Camila insisted, "Come on Jorgy, it will be fun, I promise."

And Emily warned, "But we are going out early. If you want to come, you need to be ready by 6:30 AM."

Then I remembered that Jean Gler mentioned something about Emily and practical issues. I relaxed and realized that whatever the situation will be, and whichever imaginary scenario will turn into the real one, I would probably be doing OK. "What could be so terrifying in spending the day, on the North Shore of Kauai, with two lovely girls?"

I said, "Sure, let's do it, and no worries, I will be ready at 6:30 sharp."

When Brother K, with his guitar, dedicated a song to me, and this time according to Jean Gler's request, it was "No woman no cry", I was already in the stage of realizing how lucky and happy I was, so I gladly cooperated and sang with all my heart.

Jean Gler winked at me and pointed at me when everybody sang the words *"...And Jorgy would make the fire lights..."*

I felt that this was really MY party and that everybody sang just for me.

I thought to myself, "How rare and wonderful these people are. They only met me yesterday, and now they are all singing just for me as nobody ever sang before."

CHAPTER 7

NORTH SHORE

They picked me up at 6:30 sharp, and by 6:33, as the roads were almost empty, we were already on the highway to the North Shore.

Emily was driving and seemed fully awake and focused. I sat next to her, and Camila was deeply asleep in the back seat. She was driving too fast for me, but I didn't feel comfortable to complain.

I didn't look at her directly but rather tried to steal short glances, that would hopefully look unintentional. I didn't want to be rude, or make her think that I was only interested in her physique, and didn't care about her other qualities.

I already knew she was witty, and looking at her arms while she was driving, I thought how strong she looked, which didn't surprise me at all, as I knew she was a surfer.

After a few minutes on the highway, she asked me, "Do you want to know where we are heading to?"

I didn't hesitate and said, "I trust you, and besides that, I already realized that there are no ugly places in Kauai, so I'm quite relaxed."

"Ok Jorgy, we'll surprise you, and I have no doubt

that we're going to have the most incredible day."

She wasn't an enthusiastic tourist guide like Jean Gler, however, she did show me several points of interest on the way.

It was a beautiful day. We passed through a few towns, beaches, and green mountains along the way, but I found myself dedicating my full attention to her, and I felt that she liked it.

Camila was still sleeping in the back, and seemed completely indifferent to any noise or bumps on the road.

I told Emily, "Yesterday I had some very interesting conversations with Jean Gler about investments. He shared with me many of his insights, and he also explained his Investilosophy to me. When I asked him for some practical advice on how to develop my Investilosophy, he suggested that I speak with you. He thinks highly of you."

I think she was flattered, but kept a straight face, "So you already know he is calling himself an Investilosopher. His Investilosophy works remarkably well for him. He is a gifted investor, but he tends to assume that everybody is familiar with all the terms and assumptions he uses.

"As I see it, the basic idea behind Investilosophy is simple. Investing is a personal journey. The more you learn about yourself, the better investor you become.

"Learning about yourself may sound as an easy task, but it's not. You want my practical advice?

Look for an investment questionnaire that is suitable for your investment experience and knowledge. You can find such questionnaires in investment books or websites of various service providers.

"Once you've filled out an investment questionnaire, you will have in front of you the essence of your current Investilosophy. You will then be able to develop it further, fine-tune it, or change it completely.

"If you like, I can send you a few examples of DDQs; Due Diligence Questionnaires, which Hedge Funds managers are required to fill out for prospect investors. Answering all these questions is an excellent starting point."

"Thanks, that sounds practical," I said, "but also like hard labor. What kind of questions these DDQs contain?"

Emily finally smiled and said, "Jorgy, I'm starting to believe that it's not Jean Gler's fault that you were confused, but it's your questions that require long and complicated answers. Those DDQs have anything between 20 and 200 pages, so you can imagine there are many kinds of questions, and I suggest you find out for yourself."

"Well," I said, "I guess you're right, but anyway, why does investing always have to be so complicated?"

"It really doesn't," she answered, "and that's exactly what Camila and I are doing for our living; making the investing process easier."

"Yes," I said, "I was a bit drunk, but I do remember

you were both telling me something about an Investilizer. Is it really making investing simple?"

INVESTILIZER

"Simple is maybe an overstatement," she said, "Investing is quite challenging as you know, but I would say that it makes investing easier.

I guess you've heard before the term "usability" or "user friendly"?"

"Of course," I said, "It's all over the place. I guess all industries and businesses understand that if it's friendlier and easier for the clients, they will consume more or become loyal etc."

"Well," Emily said, "I guess that in the investment industry, they didn't figure it out yet. Maybe they suffer from lack of creativity, or haven't tried hard enough yet, and that's where we come into the picture.

"We are trying to change the entire investing experience and to make it easier and even enjoyable. We develop various trading and risk management platforms. My job is to make sure that they are easy to use and functional, and our sleeping beauty, Camila, makes sure they are smooth and attractive.

"The basic idea was to make the investing process easier and accessible for the masses, so our initial products were designed for retail, non-professional investors. Now we also have institutional products. Apparently, even professional investors enjoy working with an easier and nicer interface."

"It sounds like a cool and interesting business, and that you really like what you do," I said, "congratulations! Now, let me ask you, how can "Emily" and "Camila" compete with all these financial giants? After all, they have unlimited resources: capital, talent, and infrastructure. Anyway, I think you are brave."

"Thanks," she said, "I think we get our strength and motivation from each other and from the general positive vibes in the Traders Village. And maybe some of these financial giants are satisfied with the current situation and don't want to change the world or create enjoyable trading interfaces.

"I've been there. I lived for a few years in Manhattan and built trading platforms for large Brokerage firms. I know very well how this system works.

"The financial industry has a bad reputation and for a reason. Honestly, I'm a bit tired of speaking about the corruption, lies, and conflicts of interests, but the bottom line is that the industry is not serving its purpose for investors, and I think it must change.

"We often hear that the rules of the game have changed, but nobody can say what the new rules of investing are.

"I do hope that the new rules will include some real transparency and ease of investing. When we design our trading interfaces, one of the main obstacles is the regulation.

"Take a look at various types of orders, symbols,

and terms that people need to learn if they want to invest. Check out your own daily or monthly brokerage statement and tell me that you actually understand all the terms and numbers."

"No, I don't," I interrupted, "I only look at the account value figure. The rest gives me a headache. It's not that they don't provide me with the information, it's just that I feel that I drown in it."

"Look Jorgy, it's not that I'm trying to flatter you, but you are probably smarter than the average person. Can you imagine how many people out there want to invest but just can't, because it's too complicated? What we're saying is that if it would be easier, more people could enter the investment universe, manage their money, and control their financial destiny."

ANINI BEACH

"Emily please…"

That was Camila. She woke up fuzzy like, scratching her eyes, stretching her hands, and growling. "Come on Emily, it's Sunday, can't you stop speaking about work for at least one day? Where are we anyway?"

"Good morning Princessa!" Emily greeted her. "In about 5 minutes, we'll meet your lover Anini."

"Oh really?" I tried to disguise my disappointment.

"No, not really", Emily laughed. "It's Anini Beach, and Camila calls it her lover because it is warm and calm and gentle. It is protected by a long coral reef so there are no waves, and the water is warm."

We arrived at Anini Beach and parked near the camping area. There were many tents, but it seemed like most of the people were still sleeping, as we didn't see anyone around. The ocean was flat like a swimming pool, and since it was transparent, we could clearly see the reef.

Camila pulled out of the Jeep some bread, fruits, and a blanket. We walked a bit further to the beach and sat together in silence, eating and looking at the many different shades, of turquoise and blue, of the reef.

"Jorgy, do you like Snorkeling?" Camila asked me enthusiastically.

"Yes, I think so," I replied. "I'm not a big expert, but it's fun."

"Great, so let's go. You'll take Emily's gear," Camila said decisively.

"OK, but what about Emily?" I asked and turned to look at Emily.

"Well Jorgy, you go with Camila. Snorkeling is too boring for me, and anyway, there is nothing exciting in the water here to see."

Camila came back with the gear, and we went together into the water. Before we entered, she pointed out to the different colors in the reef and explained to me which is what; corals, seaweed, shallow water, and deep blue water. She also showed me where the channel, through which we'll go outside of the reef, is.

We began our underwater journey, and I let Camila lead.

The visibility was good, but there weren't too many fish to see.

Every time I saw something interesting, I pointed at it for Camila to see, and she did the same. I touched Camila's leg when I saw a large group of Surgeonfish, and she touched mine, pointing at a sweet couple of Trumpetfish that looked as they were kissing.

She then took us through the channel into the deep blue water.

We didn't see any turtles or dolphins. Besides, I was too busy looking at the prettiest amphibian creature, Camila. She was moving so gently and looked so relaxed, and she was wearing a Brazilian Bikini.

All of a sudden Camila disappeared, and I was lost in the deep water. I was confused as I wasn't sure where exactly we came from. I wasn't in panic or anything like that, but I thought that I should swim back to the beach, with extra caution not to bump into the corals.

Then I felt something touching me and I was startled for a second, without even thinking of the type of creature it might be, but then I saw Camila laughing behind her mask.

She took me by the hand and led me back into the channel. We swam together, hand by hand like a romantic couple of Dolphins. We didn't let go until we arrived back at the beach.

I thought how strange it is... How one touch of

hands can make two people feel so close, much more than any conversation.

Emily came towards us, and we all stayed in the lagoon for another hour. Playing like children, splashing, pushing, swimming, and floating on our backs.

Then Camila said she was hungry, and Emily suggested a great seafood restaurant they know in Hanalei Bay. We all agreed, but couldn't get out of the water's playground. Finally, when we did, we passed through the camping area, on our way to the jeep. It was now full of commotion.

I thought to myself how I missed camping and that I hadn't slept in a tent for years.

HANALEI BAY

On the way to the restaurant, we drove through Hanalei Bay. It has a beautiful long beach, and picturesque green mountains surrounding it.

Emily explained that Hanalei has several surfing spots, and that it's known as one of the best spots for world champion surfers, but it also has smaller waves for beginners.

"Are we going surfing?" I asked her.

"Only if you insist," she replied. "I promised Camila that today we won't abandon her for long hours, that's why we didn't bring any surfboard with us, but we can always find a friend to borrow from or rent one."

I did not insist, and we continued to the restaurant where we indulged ourselves with enormous dishes of seafood. Afterwards, we all agreed that we needed a good rest.

We arrived at the beach and placed the blanket on the sand, under a big tree, a few steps from the water, and we immediately fell asleep.

A screaming boy, desperately calling for his mother, woke me up. I looked at the water and saw a surfer catching a perfect wave. For a minute, I envied him.

Then, I looked around me. Emily to my right and Camila to my left. I thought, "I envy myself".

After a while, they both woke up. Emily complained about her back and asked if I'm any good in giving a massage, so obviously, I did my best.

Later on, we entered the water for a short swim to refresh ourselves, and off we went to our next destination.

HAENA BEACH

We gave a ride to Jacob, a sophisticated Hippie. He and his wife arrived to Kauai 2 years ago from Minneapolis and joined "The children of Shambhala", a community of hippies that lived in tents, in the state parks of Kauai.

He explained that each state park's camping area is closed one day a week, but each park is closed on a different day so basically, every week, the tribe moves to another park. They spent the past week at

Anini Beach Park, and now camp at Haena Beach Park, which was exactly where we were heading to.

He invited us to visit their camp and mentioned that if we would ever consider joining their community, we'll have to go through the reception committee, which is always comprised of an equal number of women and men.

Haena Beach Park is located at the end of the road, at the edge of the Na Pali Coast state park. From here people cross by foot to Tunnels Beach and to Ke'e Beach, where the Kalalau trail begins.

I thought about the major role the Na Pali Coast cliffs played in my trip.

It was because of the image of those magnificent cliffs that I decided to come to Kauai. The day before, at approximately the same time, I was viewing the cliffs from the Kalalau Lookout with Jean Gler. When we arrived in Haena, I couldn't see the cliffs, but I was closer to them than ever. I promised myself to hike the Kalalau trail next time I'm here.

I couldn't dwell on that for too long, because my two ladies dragged me into the water. The color of the ocean was a stunning clear turquoise, but the water was a bit rough.

Emily said that sometimes the waves here grow taller and stronger, which makes a terrific ride, but the fun is too short.

While in the water, we looked back at the spectacular steep mountains that were covered with lush green vegetation.

When we got out of the water, Jacob approached

us and invited us for coffee in the Shambhala camp.

He introduced us to his lovely hugging friends and to his lovey-dovey wife, and we sat with them for a while, drinking coffee and talking about the wonders of Kauai.

One of the friends inquired, "How long will you be staying in Haena?"

We; Emily, Camila, and I, looked at each other a bit puzzled for a few seconds and then replied together, "We don't know."

Emily, faster than the rest of us, asked, "Jorgy, what do you say? Are you in a rush? What time is your flight tomorrow?"

And then she turned to Camila, "What do you say Princessa?"

Camila responded right away, "I say cool, let's stay the night. Jorgy please, don't be a party pooper."

I was trying to think under the pressure, analyzing the various scenarios and consequences like I always do, but for some reason I just couldn't.

Then Emily asked again, "Jorgy what time is your flight tomorrow?"

I replied, "I think it's at 2:30 PM".

"No worries then," she said, "we need to be back by 10 AM, so we can get out of here early in the morning. But only if you feel like it."

"Where will we sleep?" I asked her.

"We always have a tent in the Jeep," they answered together, and Emily added, "If you need anything, it's a short ride to Hanalei."

"OK," I said, "let's stay, but I have one condition."

"What condition?" They both asked.

"You must get me an insect repellent. I hate mosquitoes."

CHAPTER 8

FLYING BACK

Together we located the tent close to the beach and arranged the blanket inside. We joined our new hippie friends for dinner, sang along for a while, and then retired to our tent.

I've been to many 5 star hotels in my life, but I never felt as "Royal" as I did, with Emily and Camila in the tent, that night.

We woke up slowly with the first light and shared the same toothbrush.

After a refreshing swim in the clear turquoise water, Emily suggested we have pancakes with pineapple and chocolate cream in Hanalei, and Camila and I gladly agreed.

During breakfast, they began asking me, for the first time, all kind of questions: about myself, my life, my business, etc.

I was just about to finish my story, when Camila interrupted me, "Why do you have to fly today? What's the rush? What's wrong with Thursday or next Monday? Stay with us, you already know we have so much fun together."

Emily agreed, "Yes, why don't you stay with us for

a few more days? After all you are your own boss. I'm sure your business won't collapse so fast. We have a big house, so you can stay with us. We are getting along so well, the 3 of us. Jean Gler and the other friends will be very glad to have you as a neighbor, and we can go surfing together."

I was already prepared to fly back in a few hours. Their questions were not without reason and provoked me into thinking about it.

Originally, I was planned to be in Hong Kong for business. I had no real vacation on my schedule, and I had never imagined, in my wildest dreams, that I would end up eating pancakes with Pineapples in Hanalei with these 2 amazing women.

I remembered a phrase I once heard in an interview with a famous investment guru, "You have to rapidly adjust to the changing environment." It made sense to me, but still, I couldn't make up my mind.

These 2 sweet girls sat there, waiting for my answer, so I had to tell them something, "Thanks girls, you are truly amazing, but I really don't know, let me think about it."

I kept thinking about it all the way back.

"Why not?" I asked myself and repeated Camila's question, "What's wrong with Thursday?" Nobody was desperately waiting for me, and nothing was that urgent.

And so I picked up my stuff from the hotel and moved in with Emily and Camila for a few days.

I have wanted to write for a long time, and I don't mean writing business presentations or e-mails, but writing something meaningful that will empower and inspire people. I never got around to it and never found an interesting subject to write about.

When we got back from the North Shore, I suddenly realized that I had found it. Finally, an inspiration.

I decided that whenever Emily and Camila are busy working, I will sit down to write. And now I can proudly say that I began.

There is a saying that keeps echoing in my head, "What happens to you, is just the beginning of the story; the end is determined by how you react to it."

I think it's true for investments and adventures. Also for love.

On Monday, when we got back from the North Shore, I postponed the flight to Thursday.

It's Wednesday evening now, and I'm asking myself again, "Should I stay a bit longer?"

To be continued…
Jorgy